# WAQF IN INDIA

## Legal and Social Dimensions

Dr.Prasanta Mujrai

# *Table of Contents*

## Introduction

"Waqf in India: Legal and Social Dimensions" offers a captivating exploration of one of the most intriguing and complex institutions in Islamic jurisprudence as it manifests in the Indian context. This thought-provoking book delves into the multifaceted world of Waqf, tracing its historical evolution from its origins in Islamic law to its current status under Indian legislation. The authors skillfully navigate the intricate legal framework surrounding Waqf properties, particularly focusing on the landmark Waqf Act of 1995 and its subsequent amendments. By examining the social, economic, and political implications of Waqf in India, the book sheds light on its role in Muslim philanthropy, community development, and the broader discourse on secularism and minority rights in a diverse society. Readers are taken on an enlightening journey through the challenges and controversies surrounding Waqf administration, from issues of property management and transparency to the delicate balance between religious endowments and secular governance. This comprehensive analysis not only provides valuable insights for legal scholars and policymakers but also sparks crucial discussions about the future of religious institutions in modern India.

# Chapter 1: Introduction to Waqf in Islam

## Definition and Concept of Waqf

Waqf, a fundamental institution in Islamic law and society, represents a unique form of charitable endowment that has played a significant role in shaping the socio-economic landscape of Muslim communities throughout history. The term "waqf" (plural: awqaf) literally translates to "detention," "stoppage," or "tying up" in Arabic. In its legal and religious context, waqf refers to the permanent dedication of property for charitable or religious purposes, with the intention of drawing closer to Allah and benefiting humanity.

The concept of waqf is rooted in the Islamic principles of charity and social welfare. It involves the voluntary relinquishment of ownership rights over an asset, typically real estate or other valuable property, for the sake of Allah and the benefit of society. The key characteristic of waqf is its perpetuity; once established, a waqf is meant to exist in perpetuity, providing ongoing benefits to its designated beneficiaries.According to Islamic jurisprudence, waqf has three main elements:

1. Ownership by Allah: The property dedicated as waqf is considered to be transferred to the ownership of Allah, removing it from the realm of human possession.

2. Extinction of the founder's right: The person establishing the waqf (known as the waqif) relinquishes their ownership and control over the dedicated property.

3. Benefit for mankind: The usufruct or benefits derived from the waqf property are directed towards charitable or religious purposes, serving the needs of the community.

The Hanafi school of Islamic law, one of the major Sunni schools of jurisprudence, defines waqf as "the extinction of the appropriator's ownership in the thing dedicated and the detention of the thing in the implied ownership of God, in such a manner that its profits may revert to or be applied for the benefit of mankind". This definition emphasizes the transfer of ownership to Allah and the dedication of the property's benefits for human welfare.

The legal framework of waqf has been codified in various Muslim-majority countries. For instance, the Wakf Act of 1954 in India defines waqf as "the permanent dedication by a person professing Islam of any movable or immovable property for any purpose recognized by Muslim law as religious, pious, or charitable". This definition highlights the religious nature of waqf and its broad scope in terms of the types of property that can be dedicated.

It is important to note that while waqf shares some similarities with the concept of trusts in Western legal systems, it has distinct features rooted in Islamic principles. Unlike trusts, waqf is considered an act of worship ('ibadah) and is governed by specific rules derived from Islamic law.

## Historical Origin of Waqf

The institution of waqf, while not explicitly mentioned in the Quran, finds its roots in the early days of Islam and the teachings of Prophet Muhammad. The concept evolved from the Islamic emphasis on charity and the importance of using one's wealth for the benefit of others.

The earliest known instance of waqf in Islamic history is attributed to Umar ibn al-Khattab, the second Caliph of Islam. According to a hadith, Umar approached the Prophet Muhammad seeking advice on how to use a valuable piece of land he had acquired. The Prophet advised him to make the land inalienable and dedicate its proceeds to charity. This incident is often cited as the foundation for the development of the waqf system.

While some researchers suggest that the earliest waqfs providing public services may have emerged about a century after the advent of Islam, there is evidence that the term "waqf" was used by Islamic theologians from the very beginning of the Islamic state[6]. During the early Islamic period, the concept of waqf was applied to valuable conquered lands that were permanently designated to provide services to the entire Muslim community.

The juridical system of waqf began to take shape during the 2nd and 3rd Islamic centuries, around the year 755 CE. This period saw an increase in privately administered endowments established to provide public services that were previously provided by the early Islamic state through property seized from non-Muslims or taxes collected as Zakat.The development of waqf as a widespread institution was influenced by various factors, including:

1. Religious motivation: The desire to perform charitable acts and gain spiritual rewards in the afterlife.

2. Social prestige: Establishing a waqf was viewed as a spiritual act that enhanced the founder's status in the community.

3. Economic considerations: Waqf provided a means to protect property from arbitrary seizure by rulers and to ensure its continued use for beneficial purposes.

4. Public welfare: The need for sustainable funding mechanisms for public services and infrastructure.

By the Ottoman period (14th-20th centuries), the waqf system had become so extensive that it financed a wide range of public services, including health, education, and welfare. The significance of waqf in Ottoman society is illustrated by the saying that "a person would have resided in a waqf house, slept in a waqf cradle, ate and drank from waqf properties, read waqf books, taught in a waqf school, received his salary from a waqf administration, and eventually when he died, he would be put into a waqf coffin and buried in a waqf cemetery".

**Types of Waqf: Public and Private**

Waqf institutions can be broadly categorized into two main types: public waqf and private waqf. Each type serves different purposes and has distinct characteristics.

**Public Waqf**

Public waqf, also known as waqf khayri or charitable waqf is established for the benefit of the general public or a significant segment of society. The primary purpose of a public waqf is to serve religious or charitable objectives, promoting public welfare without restriction to specific family or individual beneficiaries.Characteristics of public waqf include:

1. Broad beneficiary base: The benefits are intended to reach as many people as possible within the community.

2. Religious or charitable focus: Public waqfs often support mosques, schools, hospitals, and other institutions that serve the community at large.

3. Stricter regulatory oversight: Due to their broader societal impact, public waqfs are subject to more stringent regulations and monitoring.

4. Management by statutory bodies: The administration of public waqfs typically falls under the purview of state Waqf Boards or similar governmental institutions.

Examples of public waqf include:

- Mosques and religious institutions
- Educational facilities such as schools and universities
- Healthcare facilities like hospitals and clinics
- Public infrastructure such as roads, bridges, and water supplies

## Private Waqf

Private Waqf, also known as waqf ahli, waqf dhurri, or waqf-ul-al-aulad, is created primarily for the benefit of the waqif's (founder's) family and descendants. This form of waqf functions as a family settlement structured within the framework of Islamic waqf law. Key features of private waqf include:

1. Limited beneficiary scope: The beneficiaries are typically restricted to the waqif's family members and descendants, as specified in the waqf deed.

2. Family-oriented purpose: The primary aim is to provide for the welfare and financial security of the founder's family across generations.

3. Potential charitable provisions: While primarily benefiting the founder's family, a private waqf may include provisions for charitable purposes after the extinction of the family line.

4. Legal limitations: Private Waqfs are subject to specific legal provisions to prevent perpetuities and ensure compliance with Islamic principles.

It's worth noting that some jurisdictions have placed restrictions on the creation of new private waqfs due to concerns about their potential misuse and the perpetuation of wealth inequality. However, existing private waqfs continue to operate in many Muslim-majority countries.

In addition to these two main categories, there are other specialized types of waqf, such as:

- Waqf al-sabil: Established for the benefit of the general public, particularly for the construction and maintenance of public utilities.
- Waqf al-awaridh: Created to address unforeseen circumstances or emergencies within the community.

The diversity of waqf types reflects the flexibility of the

institution in addressing various social, economic, and religious needs within Islamic societies.

## Role of Waqf in Islamic Societies

Throughout Islamic history, waqf has played a crucial role in shaping the socio-economic landscape of Muslim communities. Its impact has been far-reaching, touching various aspects of society, from religious and educational institutions to social welfare and economic development.

## Religious and Educational Sphere

One of the most significant contributions of waqf has been in the realm of religious and educational institutions. Waqf endowments have historically funded the construction and maintenance of mosques, madrasas (religious schools), and Islamic centers. These institutions have been instrumental in preserving and propagating Islamic knowledge and culture.

In the educational sector, waqf-funded schools and universities have provided access to education for countless individuals, including those from underprivileged backgrounds. The famous Al-Azhar University in Cairo, one of the oldest continuously operating universities in the world, was initially established as a waqf and continues to benefit from waqf endowments.

## Social Welfare and Poverty Alleviation

Waqf has been a powerful tool for addressing social issues and alleviating poverty in Muslim societies. Waqf-funded institutions have provided a wide range of social services, including:

- Healthcare: Hospitals, clinics, and medical schools supported by waqf endowments have provided free or low-cost medical care to communities.
- Orphanages and care for the elderly: Waqf-supported institutions have cared for vulnerable members of

society.

- Public infrastructure: Waqf funds have been used to construct and maintain public amenities such as roads, bridges, and water supplies.

These services have played a crucial role in improving the quality of life for many and reducing the burden on state resources.

## Economic Development

The waqf system has contributed significantly to economic development in Muslim societies:

1. Job creation: Waqf institutions have created employment opportunities, from administrative positions to specialized roles in various sectors.

2. Microfinance: Some waqf institutions have provided interest-free loans or grants to support small businesses and entrepreneurs.

3. Agricultural development: Waqf lands have been used for agricultural purposes, contributing to food security and rural development.

4. Urban development: Waqf properties have played a role in shaping urban landscapes, with many historic city centers in the Muslim world featuring waqf-funded buildings and institutions.

## Civil Society and Governance

Waqf has played a crucial role in the development of civil society in Muslim lands. By providing an avenue for private individuals to contribute to public welfare, waqf has fostered a sense of civic responsibility and community engagement.

Moreover, the waqf system has historically served as a check on state power. By providing essential services independently of the state, waqf institutions have helped to distribute power and resources more broadly within society.

## Challenges and Contemporary Relevance

Despite its historical significance, the waqf system faced challenges in the modern era, including mismanagement, corruption, and the encroachment of colonial and post-colonial state structures on waqf properties. However, there has been a renewed interest in reviving and reforming the waqf system in recent years.Contemporary efforts to revitalize waqf includes:

1. Legal reforms to modernize waqf administration

2. Integration of waqf with modern financial instruments, such as cash waqf and waqf-based sukuk (Islamic bonds)

3. Use of technology to improve waqf management and transparency

4. Exploration of new waqf models to address contemporary social and economic challenges

These efforts aim to harness the potential of waqf as a sustainable funding mechanism for social development and welfare in the 21st century.

## References:


1.      https://waqf.org/what-is-waqf/
2.      https://en.wikipedia.org/wiki/Waqf
3.      https://lawbhoomi.com/waqf-in-muslim-law/
4.      https://africanphilanthropy.issuelab.org/resources/20358/20358.pdf
5.      https://blog.ipleaders.in/concept-waqf-muslim-law/
6.      https://journals.iium.edu.my/intdiscourse/index.php/id/article/download/1264/832
7.      https://www.drishtijudiciary.com/editorial/waqf
8.      https://forum.albaraka.site/role-of-waqf-in-socio-economic-development/?lang=en

9.	https://www.sunlife.co.id/en/life-moments/preparing-to-retire/what-is-waqf-its-laws-types-and-virtues/

# Chapter 2: Historical Development of Waqf in India

## Historical Development of Waqf in India

The institution of Waqf has played a significant role in the socio-economic and religious landscape of India for centuries. This chapter explores the historical development of Waqf in India, tracing its evolution from the Mughal period through British colonial rule and into the post-independence era.

## Waqf During the Mughal Period

The concept of Waqf in India can be traced back to the early days of the Delhi Sultanate. One of the earliest recorded instances of Waqf in India was during the reign of Sultan Muizuddin Sam Ghaor (Muhammad Ghori), who dedicated two villages to the Jama Masjid of Multan. This act set a precedent for future rulers and wealthy individuals to establish Waqfs for religious and charitable purposes.

As the Delhi Sultanate and subsequent Islamic dynasties flourished in India, the number of Waqf properties increased significantly. The practice of creating Waqfnamas (endowment deeds) gained prominence during the reign of Firoz Shah Tughlaq (1351-1388). Firoz Shah Tughlaq is credited with organizing and promoting Waqf initiatives among the populace. During his reign, he established a hospital and appointed physicians and doctors to provide free treatment to all, supported by properties dedicated as Waqf.

The Waqf system saw further refinement during the time of Sher Shah Suri (1529-1540). According to historical accounts, Sher Shah Suri encouraged villagers to build mosques themselves, endowing plots of land for this purpose. He also established approximately 1,700 musafir khanas (rest houses) during his reign, which provided accommodation and sustenance to travelers from all parts of the country, all administered under the Waqf system.

Emperor Jalaluddin Akbar (1556-1605) made significant contributions to the enhancement of the Waqf system, focusing particularly on the upkeep of Waqf properties. Under his rule, luxurious buildings were constructed on Waqf lands, further enriching the assets of these charitable endowments.

The Mughal period saw a significant expansion of Waqf properties across India. Waqfs were established for various purposes, including mosques, madrasas (educational institutions), hospitals, and public welfare projects. This period laid the foundation for the extensive network of Waqf properties that would later become a subject of legal and administrative reforms in the colonial and post-colonial periods.

**British Colonial Policies on Waqf**

The advent of British rule in India brought significant changes to the administration and legal status of Waqf properties. Initially, the British authorities attempted to maintain the existing systems of religious endowments, including Waqfs. However, as their control over India strengthened, they introduced various laws and policies that had profound effects on the Waqf institution.

In 1810, the British passed a law for areas under Fort William of Calcutta to oversee Waqf properties. This was followed by a similar law in 1817 for areas under Fort St. George, Madras. In 1818, the supervision of Waqf properties was entrusted to the Board of Revenue and Board of Commissioners. These early laws marked the beginning of British intervention in Waqf administration.

A significant development occurred in 1863 when all previous laws were repealed, and religious Waqfs were placed under the jurisdiction of mutawallis (administrators), while the government retained the management of remaining Waqf properties. This change reflected the British policy of non-interference in religious matters while maintaining control over properties of economic significance.

The late 19th century saw legal challenges to the institution of Waqf. In 1873, the Bombay High Court issued a ruling against 'Waqf Alal Aulad', a type of Waqf established for future generations. This decision was later upheld by the Privy Council in 1894, potentially threatening the existence of many Waqfs in India.

However, the Muslim community in India strongly opposed these legal decisions. The agitation for the protection of Waqfs led to the enactment of the Mussalman Waqf Validating Act of 1913. This Act was crucial in preserving the institution of Waqf in India and marked a significant victory for the Muslim community in protecting their religious endowments.

The Mussalman Waqf Act of 1923 was another important piece of legislation during the British period. This Act attempted to regulate Waqf administration more comprehensively and remained in force until after India's independence.

The British colonial period was characterized by a gradual dismantling of the traditional Waqf system. Waqf properties were often sold and transferred as personal assets, and British policies led to the destruction and usurpation of many Waqf properties. This period of decline and legal challenges set the stage for the reforms and developments that would occur in the post-independence era.

## Post-Independence Developments in Waqf Administration

After India gained independence in 1947, the management of Waqf properties initially remained under the Mussalman Waqf Act of 1923. However, the new government soon recognized the need for comprehensive legislation to address the challenges facing Waqf administration in the post-partition context.

In 1954, the Indian Parliament passed the Waqf Act, which marked a significant shift in Waqf administration. This Act provided a pathway toward the centralization of Waqfs and established the Central Waqf Council of India as a statutory body. The 1954 Act also created state Waqf Boards with wide-ranging powers to oversee Waqf properties.

The Waqf Act of 1954 repealed several earlier laws, including the Religious Endowments Act of 1863, the Charitable Endowments Act of 1890, the Charitable and Religious Trusts Act of 1920, and the Mussalman Waqf Act of 1923. This consolidation of laws under a single Act represented a significant change in the legal framework governing Waqf administration in India.

In response to ongoing issues with the 1954 Act, the government established the Wakf Inquiry Committee to review Waqf administration. Based on the committee's recommendations, the Wakf (Amendment) Act of 1984 was introduced. This amendment aimed to restructure and improve the management of Waqf properties. Key provisions of the 1984 Amendment included the reconstitution of Waqf Boards, granting them additional powers, and the establishment of Waqf Tribunals to resolve disputes related to Waqf properties.

A major overhaul of Waqf legislation came with the Waqf Act of 1995, which replaced the 1954 Act. The 1995 Act made Waqf law an overriding law and further expanded the powers of Waqf Boards. It allowed Waqf Boards to classify properties under secular laws as Waqf, a provision that has been subject to criticism for potential overreach.

The 1995 Act also introduced the position of a Chief Executive Officer (CEO) for Waqf Boards, centralizing administrative control. The CEO, who must be Muslim, oversees Waqf properties and manages day-to-day operations. This Act also designated Waqf officials, including mutawallis, as public servants, granting those privileges and immunities under the Indian Penal Code.

In 2013, further amendments were made to the Waqf Act, strengthening the powers of Waqf Boards and addressing issues related to the management and protection of Waqf properties. These amendments aimed to improve the efficiency and transparency of Waqf administration in India.

## Waqf Contributions to Indian Society

Throughout its history in India, the institution of Waqf has made significant contributions to society, particularly in the realms of education, healthcare, and social welfare. During the Mughal period, Waqfs played a crucial role in establishing and maintaining educational institutions, hospitals, and public infrastructure.

One notable example is the Madrasa Firozshahi, established during the reign of Firoz Shah Tughlaq, which was considered one of the finest educational institutions of its time. Such institutions, supported by Waqf endowments, contributed significantly to the intellectual and cultural development of society.

The establishment of hospitals and healthcare facilities through Waqf endowments also played a crucial role in providing medical services to the public. The hospital established by Firoz Shah Tughlaq, which provided free treatment to all, is a prime example of how Waqfs contributed to public health.

In the realm of social welfare, the musafir khanas (rest houses) established by Sher Shah Suri demonstrate how Waqfs were used to provide essential services to travelers and the general public. These rest houses, numbering around 1,700, served as important infrastructure for trade and communication across the country.

In contemporary India, Waqf properties continue to play a significant role in supporting religious, educational, and charitable activities within the Muslim community. Waqf boards control approximately 8.7 lakh properties spanning 9.4 lakh acres across India, with an estimated value of Rs 1.2 lakh crore. These properties include mosques, dargahs, graveyards, madrasas, and various charitable institutions.

However, the management and utilization of Waqf properties have faced challenges, including issues of encroachment, illegal leases, and sales. The various legislative measures taken in the post-independence period have aimed to address these challenges and improve the administration of Waqf properties to ensure they continue to serve their intended charitable purposes.

**References**


1.      Brader, T. (2006). Campaigning for hearts and minds: How emotional appeals in political ads work. University of Chicago Press.

2.      Denhart, H. (2008). Deconstructing barriers: Perceptions of students labeled with learning disabilities in higher education. Journal of Learning Disabilities, 41(6), 483-497. https://doi.org/10.1177/0022219408321151

3.      Farley, B., & Small, D. (2009). Device and method for an electronic tag game (U.S. Patent No. 7,632,187). U.S. Patent and Trademark Office. https://patents.google.com/patent/US7632187B1

4.      Miller, T. E., & Schuh, J. H. (2005). Promoting reasonable expectations: Aligning student and institutional views of the college experience. Jossey-Bass.

5.      Newman, J. L., Fuqua, D. R., Gray, E. A., & Simpson, D. B. (2006). Gender differences in the relationship of anger and depression in a clinical sample. Journal of Counseling & Development, 84, 157-161.

6.      Von Busch, O., & Palmas, K. (2016). Designing

consent: Can design thinking manufacture democratic capitalism? Organizational Aesthetics, 5(2), 10-24. http://digitalcommons.wpi.edu/oa/

# Chapter 3: Legal Framework Governing Waqf in India

## Overview of the Waqf Act, 1995

The Waqf Act, 1995, stands as a cornerstone in the legal framework governing waqf properties in India. Enacted on November 22, 1995, this comprehensive legislation aims to provide better administration and supervision of waqfs, waqf properties, and all matters related to waqf. The Act replaced its predecessor, the Waqf Act of 1954, which had undergone multiple amendments to address various interpretational issues.The primary objectives of the Waqf Act, 1995 include:

1. Improving the administration and management of waqf properties

2. Establishing and facilitating the smooth functioning of the Central Waqf Council and State Waqf Boards

3. Distributing power between Chief Executive Officers and Waqf Boards

4. Regulating judicial proceedings related to waqfs

5. Supervising the powers, functions, and duties of mutawallis

6. Making the alienation of waqf property more difficult

## Key Provisions of the Waqf Act, 1995

## Definition and Creation of Waqf

The Act defines waqf as an endowment of movable or immovable property for purposes considered pious, religious, or charitable under Muslim law. It allows for the creation of waqf through three methods:

1. Declaration

2. Recognition based on long-term use (waqf by user)

3. Endowment when the line of succession ends (waqf-alal-aulad)

## Administrative Structure

The Act establishes a hierarchical administrative structure for waqf management:

1. Central Waqf Council: Advises the central and state governments and Waqf Boards

2. State Waqf Boards: Manage waqf properties within their respective states

3. Chief Executive Officers: Assist in the administration of waqfs

## Survey and Registration of Waqf Properties

The Act mandates the appointment of a Survey Commissioner to conduct surveys and identify waqf properties. It also requires the mandatory registration of all waqfs with the Waqf Board and the maintenance of a central register of waqfs.

## Financial Management

The Act introduces measures to strengthen financial management of waqf properties, including:

1. Preparation of annual budgets for waqf maintenance

2. Maintenance of records and inspection of waqf properties

3. Appointment of executive officers for underperforming waqfs with annual incomes exceeding Rs 5 lakh

## Dispute Resolution

The Act establishes Waqf Tribunals to adjudicate disputes related to waqf properties. These tribunals are deemed civil courts with powers similar to those exercised under the Code of Civil Procedure, 1908.

## Amendments to the Waqf Laws

Since its enactment, the Waqf Act, 1995 has undergone several amendments to address emerging challenges and improve its effectiveness. The most significant recent amendment is the Waqf (Amendment) Bill, 2024, which introduces substantial changes to the existing law.

## The Waqf (Amendment) Bill, 2024

Introduced in the Indian Lok Sabha on August 8, 2024, this bill proposes several key amendments to enhance transparency, accountability, and inclusivity in waqf administration.

## Renaming the Act

The bill renames the Waqf Act, 1995 to the "United Waqf Management, Empowerment, Efficiency and Development Act, 1995" (UWMEEDA 1995), reflecting its broader objectives.

## Changes in Waqf Formation and Property Classification

1. The bill restricts waqf formation to individuals practicing Islam for at least five years and clarifies that the person must own the property being declared.

2. It removes the concept of "waqf by user" and modifies waqf-alal-aulad to ensure inheritance rights for all heirs, including women.

3. Government properties identified as waqf will cease to be so, with the District Collector determining ownership in cases of uncertainty.

## Administrative Reforms

1. The bill empowers Collectors to conduct surveys of waqf properties, replacing the role of Survey Commissioners.

2. It provides for a broader composition of the Central Waqf Council and State Waqf Boards, ensuring representation of Muslim women and non-Muslims.

3. The bill establishes separate Boards of Auqaf for Boharas and Aghakhanis.

## Enhanced Transparency and Accountability

1. The bill introduces mandatory verification for all waqf property claims.

2. It streamlines the registration of waqfs through a central portal and database.

3. The Central government is granted authority to order audits of waqf properties.

## Dispute Resolution Reforms

1. The bill reforms the Tribunal structure, providing for two members and appeals to the High Court within 90 days.

2. It omits sections 108 and 108A, making the Limitation Act, 1963 applicable to actions under the Act.

These amendments aim to address concerns over arbitrary powers of Waqf Boards and prevent misuse of waqf properties.

## Role of Indian Judiciary in Waqf Matters

The Indian judiciary, particularly the Supreme Court, has played a crucial role in interpreting and shaping waqf laws. Through various judgments, the courts have clarified key aspects of waqf administration and jurisdiction.

## Jurisdiction of Waqf Boards and Tribunals

In a significant ruling, the Supreme Court held that the original jurisdiction to decide issues pertaining to Mutawalliship (trusteeship) vests with the Waqf Board and not the Waqf Tribunal. The Court distinguished between the roles of Waqf Boards and Tribunals:

1. Waqf Boards: Deal with administration-related issues, including the appointment and removal of mutawallis.

2. Waqf Tribunals: Act as adjudicatory authorities over disputes.

This clarification helps streamline the decision-making process in waqf administration and dispute resolution.

## Jurisdiction of Waqf Tribunals

The Supreme Court has also clarified the scope of Waqf Tribunal jurisdiction. In a landmark judgment, the Court held that a Waqf Tribunal has jurisdiction to adjudicate a dispute even if a property is admitted to be a waqf property. This ruling addressed the confusion arising from earlier judgments that suggested Tribunals only had jurisdiction when the waqf status of a property was disputed.

## The Court observed:

"To say that the Tribunal will have jurisdiction only if the subject property is disputed to be a waqf property and not if it is admitted to be a waqf property, is indigestible in the teeth of Section 83".

This interpretation ensures that Waqf Tribunals can effectively adjudicate a wide range of disputes related to waqf properties, promoting more efficient resolution of waqf-related issues.

## Waqf Tribunals and Their Jurisdiction

Waqf Tribunals play a crucial role in the legal framework governing waqf in India. Established under the Waqf Act, 1995, these tribunals are designed to provide specialized adjudication for waqf-related disputes.

## Powers and Functions of Waqf Tribunals

Waqf Tribunals are vested with significant powers and functions:

1. Civil Court Status: Waqf Tribunals are deemed to be civil courts and are required to exercise all the powers and functions of a civil court under the Code of Civil Procedure, 1908.

2. Finality of Decisions: The decisions of a Waqf Tribunal are final and binding on the parties involved. No suit or legal proceedings can be initiated in any civil court against these decisions.

3. Jurisdiction over Various Matters: Waqf Tribunals have jurisdiction over a wide range of issues related to waqf properties, including disputes about the waqf status of properties, management issues, and rights of mutawallis.

## Scope of Jurisdiction

The Supreme Court's interpretations have significantly clarified and expanded the scope of Waqf Tribunal jurisdiction:

1. Admitted Waqf Properties: Waqf Tribunals have jurisdiction even over properties that are admittedly waqf properties, not just those whose waqf status is disputed.

2. Types of Remedies: The Court has outlined that three types of remedies can be sought before a Waqf Tribunal: suits, applications, and appeals.

3. Aggrieved Persons: The 2013 amendment to the Waqf Act expanded the category of persons who can approach the Tribunal from "any person interested" to "any person aggrieved," potentially including non-Muslims.

## Matters Adjudicated by Waqf Tribunals

Based on the Supreme Court's interpretations, Waqf Tribunals can adjudicate the following matters:

1. Disputes regarding the status of properties as waqf properties

2. Rights of mutawallis or beneficiaries

3. Succession to the office of mutawalli

4. Fixation of rent of waqf properties

5. Eviction of tenants from waqf properties

6. Removal of encroachments from waqf properties

7. Grant of sanction for alienation of waqf properties

8. Institution of legal proceedings on behalf of waqf

9. Commutation of cash grants

10. Release of waqf properties from enemy property status

11. Determination of rights in or over waqf properties

This comprehensive jurisdiction ensures that Waqf Tribunals can effectively address a wide range of issues related to waqf administration and management.

**References:**


1. https://www.business-standard.com/india-news/decoded-how-is-a-waqf-created-and-what-are-the-powers-of-waqf-board-124080500469_1.html
2. https://www.business-standard.com/india-news/what-are-the-key-amendments-in-waqf-act-amendment-bill-key-details-124080500310_1.html
3. https://www.livelaw.in/supreme-court/waqf-board-not-waqf-tribunal-has-jurisdiction-to-appoint-mutawalli-supreme-court-255468
4. https://pib.gov.in/PressNoteDetails.aspx?NoteId=152139&ModuleId=3
5. https://en.wikipedia.org/wiki/The_Waqf_(Amendment)_Bill,_2024
6. https://www.livelaw.in/top-stories/supreme-court-waqf-tribunal-jurisdiction-admitted-waqf-property-184812
7. https://blog.ipleaders.in/understanding-the-essential-provisions-of-the-waqf-act-1995/
8. https://economictimes.indiatimes.com/news/india/waqf-act-amendments-tighter-control-more-women-and-non-muslims-members-five-key-changes-to-waqf-

law/articleshow/112373521.cms

___

# Chapter 4: Administration of Waqf Properties in India

The administration of Waqf properties in India is a complex system involving multiple stakeholders and regulatory bodies. This chapter examines the key components of Waqf administration, including the Central Waqf Council, State Waqf Boards, challenges in asset management, and the role of Waqf managers and trustees.

## Central Waqf Council: Functions and Limitations

The Central Waqf Council (CWC) is a statutory body established under the Waqf Act of 1954 to provide oversight and guidance for the administration of Waqf properties across India. Created in 1964, the CWC operates under the Ministry of Minority Affairs and serves as the primary advisory body to the central government, state governments, and Waqf Boards on matters related to Waqf management.

## Functions of the Central Waqf Council

The CWC performs several crucial functions in the administration of Waqf properties:

1. Advisory Role: The council advises the central government on matters concerning the working of Waqf Boards and the administration of Waqfs throughout the country.

2. Issuance of Directives: The CWC is authorized to issue directives to State Waqf Boards regarding financial aspects of Waqf management, including property maintenance, deed execution, and revenue record examination.

3. Legal Guidance: It provides legal advice to the central government and state Waqf boards on protecting and recovering Waqf properties.

4. Fund Management: The council governs and maintains the

Central Waqf Fund.

5. Financial Oversight: It keeps and maintains books of accounts as prescribed by the central government.

6. Supervision: The CWC supervises and regulates the working and administration of state Waqf boards.

**Composition of the Central Waqf Council**

The CWC's composition is designed to ensure representation from various sectors and expertise:

1. Chairperson: The Union Minister in charge of Waqfs serves as the ex-officio chairperson.

2. Members: The council consists of up to 20 members appointed by the central government, all of whom must be Muslims.

3. Representation: Members include Muslim members of Parliament, persons with expertise in Waqf administration, and representatives from Muslim organizations.

4. Gender Representation: At least two members of the council must be women.

5. Executive Head: A secretary is appointed as the executive head to manage day-to-day functions and implement provisions of the Waqf Act.

**Limitations of the Central Waqf Council**

Despite its broad mandate, the CWC faces several limitations in its functioning:

1. Advisory Nature: As primarily an advisory body, the CWC's recommendations are not binding on state Waqf boards or the central government.

2. Limited Executive Powers: The council lacks direct executive authority over state Waqf boards, which can hinder the implementation of its directives.

3. Coordination Challenges: With 32 Waqf boards across states and union territories, ensuring uniform implementation of policies and practices remains a challenge.

4. Resource Constraints: The CWC may face limitations in terms of financial and human resources to effectively oversee the vast network of Waqf properties across the country.

## State Waqf Boards: Structure and Responsibilities

State Waqf Boards are the primary bodies responsible for the direct administration and management of Waqf properties within their respective states.

## Structure of State Waqf Boards

The composition of State Waqf Boards typically includes:

1. Chairperson: Appointed by the state government to oversee the board's activities.

2. Members: The board comprises several members appointed by the government, including:

- Representatives from the Muslim community
- Muslim legislators and parliamentarians
- Members of the state Bar Council
- Islamic scholars
- Mutawalis (managers) of Waqfs with an annual income of Rs 1 lakh and above.

3. Secretary: Responsible for administrative functions and acts as the primary point of contact.

## Responsibilities of State Waqf Boards

State Waqf Boards have a wide range of responsibilities in managing Waqf properties:

1. Property Administration: They are responsible for administering Waqf properties, including maintenance,

development, and ensuring proper utilization.

2. Recovery of Lost Properties: Boards are tasked with identifying and recovering Waqf properties that may have been lost or encroached upon.

3. Property Transfers: They sanction the transfer of immovable Waqf properties through sale, gift, mortgage, exchange, or lease, with at least two-thirds of board members voting in favor.

4. Appointment of Custodians: Boards appoint custodians to ensure that Waqfs and their revenues are used for their designated purposes.

5. Registration and Record-Keeping: They maintain a central register of Waqfs and ensure proper registration of all Waqf properties.

6. Financial Management: Boards prepare annual budgets for Waqf maintenance and oversee financial aspects of Waqf administration.

7. Legal Representation: State Waqf Boards can sue and be sued in court, acting as legal entities capable of acquiring, holding, and transferring property.

## Challenges in Managing Waqf Assets

The administration of Waqf properties in India faces numerous challenges that hinder effective management and utilization of these assets:

1. Legal Issues: The principle of "once a Waqf, always a Waqf" has led to various disputes and claims, some of which have been deemed perplexing by courts. The irrevocability of Waqf properties can complicate management and development efforts.

2. Encroachment and Mismanagement: Many Waqf properties face issues of encroachment, mismanagement, and ownership

disputes. The lack of effective coordination with local revenue authorities exacerbates these problems.

3. Litigation: The Waqf Act, 1995, and its 2013 amendment have been criticized for inefficacy, leading to a large number of pending cases. As of recent reports, there are 40,951 cases pending in Waqf tribunals.

4. Limited Judicial Oversight: The absence of judicial oversight on tribunal decisions complicates Waqf management. Without the possibility of appealing to a higher judicial body, decisions made by tribunals may undermine transparency and accountability.

5. Financial Constraints: Many Waqf properties generate low income due to factors such as low rental rates and limited investment strategies. This lack of funds hinders proper maintenance and development of Waqf assets.

6. Incomplete Records: Incomplete or obsolete data on Waqf properties makes it difficult to manage and protect these assets effectively.

7. Management Inefficiencies: Issues such as lack of professional expertise, inadequate staffing, and poor coordination between trustees contribute to inefficient management of Waqf properties.

8. Awareness and Knowledge Gap: There is often a lack of awareness and knowledge about Waqf practices among both managers and the general public, leading to underutilization of Waqf potential.

9. Idle Assets: Many Waqf properties, even those in strategic locations, remain undeveloped due to various constraints, including financial limitations and management issues.

10. Illegal Invasion: Unauthorized occupation or use of Waqf properties is a persistent problem that diminishes the value and

utility of these assets.

## Role of Waqf Managers and Trustees

Waqf managers and trustees, also known as mutawalis, play a crucial role in the day-to-day administration of Waqf properties:

1. Property Management: Mutawalis are responsible for the direct management of Waqf properties, ensuring their maintenance and proper utilization.

2. Financial Administration: They oversee the financial aspects of Waqf management, including collecting rents, managing expenses, and maintaining accounts.

3. Compliance with Waqf Objectives: Managers must ensure that the Waqf properties are used in accordance with the intentions of the Waqif (founder) and comply with Islamic principles.

4. Reporting: They are required to maintain proper records and report to the State Waqf Boards on the status and activities of the Waqf properties under their management.

5. Development Initiatives: Mutawalis may propose and implement development projects to enhance the value and utility of Waqf properties, subject to approval from the Waqf Board.

6. Legal Representation: In some cases, managers may represent the Waqf in legal matters, working in coordination with the State Waqf Board.

7. Community Engagement: Waqf managers often serve as a link between the Waqf institution and the local community, ensuring that the benefits of the Waqf reach the intended beneficiaries.

However, the role of Waqf managers and trustees is not without challenges:

1. Skill Gap: Many mutawalis lack the professional and technical

expertise required for effective property management and development.

2. Resource Constraints: Limited financial and human resources often hinder the ability of managers to effectively administer Waqf properties.

3. Accountability Issues: There have been instances of misuse of power by mutawalis, highlighting the need for better oversight and accountability mechanisms.

4. Succession Planning: Ensuring continuity in management and preserving institutional knowledge can be challenging, especially when competent managers leave their positions.

**References:**


1. https://www.pw.live/exams/upsc/waqf-board/
2. https://www.legalservicesindia.com/article/1433/Administration-of-Wakf-in-India.html
3. https://pib.gov.in/PressNoteDetails.aspx?NoteId=152139&ModuleId=3
4. https://www.business-standard.com/india-news/decoded-how-is-a-waqf-created-and-what-are-the-powers-of-waqf-board-124080500469_1.html
5. https://blog.ipleaders.in/central-waqf-council/
6. https://www.studyiq.com/articles/waqf-board/
7. https://jurcon.ums.edu.my/ojums/index.php/LJMS/article/download/2868/1906/9957
8. https://economictimes.indiatimes.com/news/india/waqf-through-the-ages-how-rs-1-lakh-crore-property-owner-board-acquires-land-and-what-the-govt-aims-to-change/articleshow/112365585.cms

## *Chapter 5: Registration and Identification of Waqf Properties*

The registration and identification of waqf properties are crucial aspects of waqf management, ensuring the proper administration and protection of these charitable endowments. This chapter explores the importance of registration under waqf laws, the procedures for identifying waqf properties, disputes that arise in the registration process, and the role of technology in waqf surveys.

### Importance of Registration under Waqf Laws

The registration of waqf properties is a fundamental requirement under waqf laws, serving several critical purposes in the management and protection of these charitable endowments.

### Legal Recognition and Protection

Registration of waqf properties provides them with legal recognition and protection. According to the Waqf Act of 1995, it is mandatory to register all waqf properties at the office of the board. This legal recognition is crucial for safeguarding the property against potential encroachment, illegal occupation, or unauthorized sale. Once registered, the waqf property gains a legal status that allows it to file suits for the protection of its rights and properties.

### Transparency and Accountability

Registration promotes transparency and accountability in the management of waqf properties. By maintaining a comprehensive register of all waqf properties, the State Waqf Boards can effectively monitor and oversee their administration. This transparency helps prevent mismanagement and ensures that the properties are used in accordance with the intentions of the waqif (donor).

## Facilitation of Management

Proper registration facilitates the efficient management of waqf properties. It provides a clear record of the property's details, including its description, gross annual income, land revenue, and estimated expenses. This information is essential for the mutawalli (trustee) and the Waqf Board to make informed decisions regarding the property's maintenance, development, and utilization.

## Legal Compliance

Registration is a legal requirement under the Waqf Act, 1995. Failure to register a waqf property can lead to penalties for the mutawalli. By ensuring compliance with this legal obligation, registration helps maintain the integrity of the waqf system and prevents potential legal complications.

## Access to Benefits and Schemes

Registered waqf institutions are entitled to various benefits and schemes offered by the Waqf Board, Central Waqf Council, or government. These may include financial assistance for property development, legal aid for property protection, and access to various welfare schemes aimed at benefiting the Muslim community.

## Public Awareness and Trust

Registration contributes to public awareness about the existence and purpose of waqf properties. This transparency builds trust among stakeholders and the general public, potentially encouraging more individuals to contribute to waqf causes.

## Procedures for Identifying Waqf Properties

The identification of waqf properties involves a systematic process that ensures accurate recognition and documentation of these charitable endowments. The procedures for identifying waqf properties typically include the following steps:

**1. Initial Declaration and Documentation:** The process begins with the waqif (donor) making a clear declaration of their intention to dedicate a property as waqf. This declaration can be oral or written, but a written declaration is preferred for legal documentation. The declaration should include details of the property, its location, and the purpose of the waqf.

**2. Execution of the Waqf Deed:** A formal waqf deed is prepared, which serves as a legal document recording the creation of the waqf. This deed includes the waqif's declaration, the purpose of the waqf, details of the property involved, and the appointment of the mutawalli (trustee). The deed must be clear and precise to avoid any future ambiguities or misinterpretations.

**3. Registration with the Waqf Board:** In India, the Waqf Act, 1995 mandates the registration of waqf properties with the relevant state Waqf Board. The mutawalli or the waqif must submit the waqf deed along with other necessary documents to the Waqf Board. These documents typically include:

- Proof of ownership of the property
- Detailed description of the property
- Maps or plans of the property
- Estimated annual income and expenses
- Details of the mutawalli

The Waqf Board verifies the authenticity of the waqf and ensures that the declaration and deed comply with the law before registering the property as waqf.

**4. Government Surveys:** State governments, through the Waqf Boards, conduct periodic surveys of waqf properties. These surveys aim to identify, document, and safeguard waqf properties across the state. The survey process typically involves:

- Physical inspection of properties

- Review of historical records and documents
- Consultation with local communities and religious authorities
- Verification of property ownership and usage

**5. Publication of Survey Findings:** The results of these surveys are published in the official gazette, listing the properties that are recognized as waqf. This notification serves as official recognition of the waqf and provides public notice of its status.

**6. Maintenance of Waqf Register:** The State Waqf Boards are responsible for maintaining a comprehensive register of all waqf properties. This register includes details such as:

- Description of the waqf property
- Gross annual income of the property
- Amount of land revenue and cesses payable
- Estimated expenses for the property
- Other relevant information as prescribed by the board

## 7. Continuous Monitoring and Updating

The identification and registration of waqf properties is an ongoing process. The Waqf Boards continually monitor and update their records to ensure accuracy and completeness. This may involve:

- Regular inspections of registered properties
- Investigation of potential unregistered waqf properties
- Updating property details in case of changes or developments

## Disputes in Waqf Property Registration

The registration of waqf properties, while crucial for their proper management and protection, often gives rise to various disputes. These conflicts can arise due to several factors and can significantly impact the effective administration of waqf properties.

**Types of Disputes**

**1. Ownership Disputes:** One of the most common disputes in waqf property registration involves conflicting claims of ownership. These disputes can arise when:

- Multiple parties claim ownership of the same property
- There is a lack of clear documentation proving the waqf status of a property
- Heirs of the original waqif contest the waqf declaration

**2. Boundary Disputes:** Disputes often arise regarding the exact boundaries of waqf properties, especially in cases where:

- The original waqf deed lacks precise boundary descriptions
- Encroachments have occurred over time
- Neighboring properties have unclear demarcations

**3. Purpose and Utilization Disputes:** Conflicts can emerge regarding the intended purpose and utilization of waqf properties, particularly when:

- The original purpose of the waqf is no longer feasible or relevant
- Different stakeholders interpret the waqf's purpose differently
- There are disagreements about how the property should be utilized or developed

**4. Registration Process Disputes :** Disputes can also arise during the registration process itself, including:

- Challenges to the validity of the waqf declaration
- Disagreements about the appointment of mutawallis
- Objections to the survey and identification process

conducted by Waqf Boards

**Causes of Disputes:** Several factors contribute to the emergence of disputes in waqf property registration:

**1. Lack of Clear Documentation:** Many waqf properties, especially older ones, lack clear and comprehensive documentation. This absence of proper records can lead to confusion and conflicting claims.

**2. Misuse of Legal Provisions:** Some stakeholders may misuse legal provisions, such as Section 40 of the Waqf Act, to acquire and declare properties as waqf, leading to disputes and disharmony among communities.

**3. Ineffective Survey and Registration Processes:** Unsatisfactory survey work and delays in the registration process can lead to disputes. For instance, in some states like Gujarat and Uttarakhand, the survey of waqf properties has not even started, while in Uttar Pradesh, a survey ordered in 2014 is yet to begin.

**4. Lack of Awareness:** Many property owners and stakeholders lack awareness about waqf laws and registration procedures, leading to unintentional non-compliance and subsequent disputes.

**Resolution Mechanisms:** To address these disputes, several resolution mechanisms are in place:

**1. Waqf Tribunals:** Waqf Tribunals are established to adjudicate disputes related to waqf properties. However, the effectiveness of these tribunals has been questioned due to the lack of judicial oversight and the inability to grant stays on their decisions.

**2. Legal Reforms:** The government is considering amendments to the Waqf Act to address some of the issues leading to disputes. These reforms aim to improve the registration process and increase the role of technology in managing waqf records.

**3. Alternative Dispute Resolution:** Some states are exploring alternative dispute resolution mechanisms, such as mediation, to resolve waqf property disputes more efficiently and amicably.

**4. Improved Documentation and Surveys:** Efforts are being made to improve the documentation of waqf properties and conduct more thorough and accurate surveys to prevent future disputes.

## Role of Technology in Waqf Surveys

In the era of digital transformation, technology plays a crucial role in revolutionizing the process of waqf surveys, making them more efficient, accurate, and transparent. The integration of advanced technologies in waqf management, often referred to as "Waqf 4.0," is transforming the landscape of waqf administration.

**Digital Mapping and Geographical Information Systems (GIS):** One of the most significant technological advancements in waqf surveys is the use of digital mapping and Geographical Information Systems (GIS). These technologies offer several benefits:

1. Accurate Property Identification: GIS allows for precise mapping of waqf properties, including their boundaries and geographical features. This accuracy helps in resolving boundary disputes and preventing encroachments.

2. Spatial Analysis: GIS enables spatial analysis of waqf properties, providing insights into their distribution, accessibility, and potential for development.

3. Integration with Land Records: Digital mapping can be integrated with existing land record databases, facilitating easier verification and cross-referencing of property information.

**Blockchain Technology:** Blockchain technology is emerging as a powerful tool for waqf management, offering several advantages for property surveys and registration:

1. Immutable Records: Blockchain provides an immutable and transparent record of waqf properties, ensuring the integrity of survey data and preventing unauthorized alterations.

2. Smart Contracts: Smart contracts on blockchain platforms can automate various aspects of waqf management, including property registration and fund allocation.

3. Increased Transparency: Blockchain's decentralized nature enhances transparency in waqf management, building trust among stakeholders.

**Mobile Applications and Crowdsourcing:** Mobile applications can revolutionize the way waqf surveys are conducted:

1. Field Data Collection: Mobile apps enable surveyors to collect and upload property data in real-time, improving efficiency and reducing errors.

2. Crowdsourced Information: Apps can allow community members to report potential waqf properties or provide additional information, supplementing official surveys.

3. Public Access to Information: Mobile platforms can provide easy access to waqf property information for the public, increasing awareness and transparency.

**Artificial Intelligence and Machine Learning:** AI and machine learning technologies have the potential to enhance waqf surveys in several ways:

1. Automated Property Identification: AI algorithms can analyze satellite imagery and historical records to identify potential waqf properties that may have been overlooked.

2. Predictive Analytics: Machine learning models can predict trends in waqf property utilization and development, aiding in

strategic planning.

3. Natural Language Processing: NLP can be used to analyze historical documents and waqf deeds, extracting relevant information for property identification and classification.

**Cloud Computing and Big Data Analytics:** The use of cloud computing and big data analytics can significantly improve the management and analysis of waqf survey data:

1. Centralized Data Storage: Cloud-based systems allow for centralized storage of waqf property data, ensuring easy access and data consistency across different agencies.

2. Advanced Analytics: Big data analytics can provide insights into waqf property trends, utilization patterns, and potential areas for development.

3. Improved Decision Making: Data-driven insights can support better decision-making in waqf management and policy formulation.

**Challenges and Considerations:** While technology offers numerous benefits for waqf surveys, there are also challenges to consider:

1. Digital Divide: The implementation of advanced technologies may be hindered by the digital divide, especially in rural or underdeveloped areas.

2. Data Privacy and Security: The digitization of waqf property data raises concerns about data privacy and security, necessitating robust cybersecurity measures.

3. Training and Capacity Building: The effective use of these technologies requires training and capacity building for waqf administrators and surveyors.

4. Integration with Existing Systems: There may be challenges in integrating new technologies with existing waqf management

systems and processes.

In conclusion, the registration and identification of waqf properties are critical processes that ensure the proper management and protection of these charitable endowments. The importance of registration under waqf laws cannot be overstated, as it provides legal recognition, promotes transparency, and facilitates effective management. The procedures for identifying waqf properties involve a systematic approach, from initial declaration to official registration and continuous monitoring.

However, the process is not without challenges, as evidenced by the various disputes that can arise during waqf property registration. These disputes, ranging from ownership conflicts to disagreements about property utilization, highlight the need for clear documentation, effective survey processes, and robust dispute resolution mechanisms.

The role of technology in waqf surveys represents a promising avenue for improving the efficiency and accuracy of property identification and management. From digital mapping and blockchain to artificial intelligence and big data analytics, these technological advancements offer the potential to revolutionize waqf administration. However, their implementation must be balanced with considerations of accessibility, data security, and capacity building.

As the landscape of waqf management continues to evolve, it is crucial for stakeholders to embrace these technological advancements while addressing the challenges they present. By doing so, the administration of waqf properties can be significantly enhanced, ensuring that these charitable endowments continue to serve their intended purposes effectively in the modern era.

**References:**

1. https://blog.ipleaders.in/understanding-the-essential-provisions-of-the-waqf-act-1995/
2. https://mahawakf.com/faq/
3. https://waqf.gov.in/homepage/newRegistration.php
4. https://www.commercialnoida.com/blog/how-to-find-list-of-waqf-properties-in-india
5. https://ksandk.com/private-clients/law-relating-waqf-properties-in-india/
6. https://www.drishtijudiciary.com/current-affairs/government-to-determine-waqf-properties-under-dispute
7. https://pib.gov.in/PressNoteDetails.aspx?NoteId=152139&ModuleId=3&s=09
8. https://www.emerald.com/insight/content/doi/10.1108/jima-03-2024-0111/full/html
9. https://pib.gov.in/PressNoteDetails.aspx?NoteId=152139&ModuleId=3
10. https://rsisinternational.org/journals/ijriss/articles/revolutionizing-waqf-management-harnessing-the-fourth-industrial-revolution-for-waqf-4-0-transformation/

# Chapter 6: Litigation and Disputes in Waqf Properties

Waqf properties, which are charitable endowments under Islamic law, have been subject to numerous disputes and legal challenges in India. This chapter examines the common causes of these disputes, the role of courts and tribunals in resolving them, the impact of legal delays, and notable case laws that have shaped the jurisprudence around waqf properties.

**Common Causes of Waqf Property Disputes:** Several factors contribute to the frequent disputes surrounding waqf properties in India:

## Lack of Proper Documentation

One of the primary causes of waqf property disputes is the absence of proper documentation. Many waqf properties in India were created through oral declarations or informal written agreements, without following proper legal procedures. This lack of clear documentation often leads to disputes over the ownership and status of properties claimed as waqf.

## Encroachment and Illegal Occupation

Encroachment on waqf lands is a widespread issue. Due to the valuable nature of many waqf properties, especially those in prime urban locations, there have been numerous instances of illegal occupation and encroachment. This has led to protracted legal battles between waqf boards and encroachers.

## Mismanagement by Mutawallis

Mutawallis, who are appointed to manage waqf properties, have sometimes been accused of mismanagement or even misappropriation of waqf assets. This has resulted in disputes between waqf boards and mutawallis, as well as beneficiaries of the waqf.

## Conflicting Claims of Ownership

In some cases, multiple parties claim ownership of the same property, leading to complex legal disputes. This is often due to the historical nature of many waqf properties and the lack of clear title documents.

## Issues with Waqf Board Powers

The sweeping powers given to waqf boards to declare properties as waqf have sometimes been misused, leading to disputes with private property owners. This has been a contentious issue, especially when properties are declared waqf without sufficient evidence.

## Irrevocability of Waqf

The principle of "once a waqf, always a waqf" has led to various disputes and claims. This irrevocability has sometimes resulted in conflicts, especially when the original intention of the waqf creator is disputed.

**Role of Courts and Tribunals in Resolving Disputes:** The resolution of waqf property disputes involves various judicial bodies:

**Waqf Tribunals:** Waqf Tribunals were established under the Waqf Act, 1995 to specifically deal with disputes related to waqf properties. These tribunals have the power to adjudicate on matters such as:

- Disputes regarding the status of properties as waqf
- Removal of encroachments from waqf properties
- Recovery of waqf properties
- Disputes between waqf boards and mutawallis

The tribunals are meant to provide a specialized forum for quick resolution of waqf-related disputes. However, their effectiveness has been questioned due to delays and lack of enforcement mechanisms.

## Civil Courts

Prior to the establishment of waqf tribunals, civil courts had jurisdiction over waqf property disputes. Even now, certain matters related to waqf properties may fall under the jurisdiction of civil courts, especially when the dispute involves parties who are not Muslims or when the waqf status of a property is itself in question.

## High Courts and Supreme Court

High Courts have the power to hear appeals against decisions of waqf tribunals. The Supreme Court, being the apex court of the country, can hear appeals from High Court decisions on waqf matters. These higher courts have played a crucial role in interpreting waqf laws and setting precedents.

**Challenges in the Judicial Process:** Despite the establishment of specialized tribunals, the resolution of waqf property disputes faces several challenges:

1. Lack of clear jurisdiction: There is often confusion about whether a particular dispute should be heard by a waqf tribunal or a civil court.

2. Delays in constitution of tribunals: Many states have been slow in setting up waqf tribunals, leading to a backlog of cases.

3. Limited powers of tribunals: Waqf tribunals do not have the power to grant stay orders, which sometimes hampers their ability to provide immediate relief.

4. Absence of appellate mechanism: Decisions of waqf tribunals can only be challenged through writ petitions in High Courts, which can lead to further delays.

**Impact of Legal Delays on Waqf Properties:** The prolonged litigation surrounding waqf properties has had significant negative impacts:

## Deterioration of Properties

Many waqf properties remain unused or underutilized due to ongoing legal disputes. This often leads to the physical deterioration of these properties, some of which may have historical or architectural significance.

## Loss of Revenue

Disputes and legal uncertainties prevent the effective management and development of waqf properties. This results in a substantial loss of potential revenue that could have been used for charitable purposes as intended by the waqf creators.

## Encroachment and Illegal Occupation

Prolonged legal battles often provide opportunities for further encroachment and illegal occupation of waqf properties. The longer a dispute remains unresolved, the more difficult it becomes to reclaim the property.

## Administrative Burden

The large number of pending cases places a significant administrative burden on waqf boards and the judicial system. This diverts resources from the proper management and development of waqf properties.

## Erosion of Public Trust

The frequent disputes and allegations of mismanagement have eroded public trust in the waqf system. This can potentially discourage future waqf dedications and hamper the growth of waqf assets.

**Notable Case Laws on Waqf in India:** Several landmark judgments have shaped the legal landscape of waqf properties in India:

## Bakar Ali vs. Abu Sayid Khan (1901)

This case established important principles regarding the creation and validity of waqf. The court held that for a waqf to be valid there must be a permanent dedication of property for religious or charitable purposes recognized by Muslim law.

## M. Kazim vs. A Asghar Ali (AIR 1932)

This case clarified the legal definition of waqf, stating that it means the creation of some property for religious or charitable purposes recognized by Muslim law, where the property is dedicated in perpetuity.

## Abul Fata Mahomed Ishak and others vs. Rasamaya Dhur Chowdhuri and others (1891)

This case dealt with the issue of family waqfs. The Privy Council held that a waqf created primarily for the benefit of the creator's family, with only a remote possibility of it being used for charitable purposes, was not a valid waqf.

## Karnataka Board of Wakfs v. Mohd. Nazeer Ahmad (1982)

This case addressed the issue of what constitutes a valid waqf under Muslim law. The court held that for a waqf to be valid, it must have a religious, pious, or charitable purpose benefiting the Muslim community.

## Ramesh Gobindram vs. Sugra Humayun Mirza Wakf (2010)

This case dealt with the jurisdiction of waqf tribunals. The Supreme Court held that waqf tribunals have exclusive jurisdiction to determine disputes concerning waqf properties, even if one of the parties is not a Muslim. These case laws have played a crucial role in interpreting waqf laws, defining the scope of waqf boards' powers, and establishing principles for resolving waqf property disputes.

In conclusion, the litigation and disputes surrounding waqf

properties in India present complex challenges that require a multifaceted approach. While the establishment of specialized tribunals was intended to expedite dispute resolution, issues of jurisdiction, delays, and enforcement continue to plague the system. The impact of these legal battles on waqf properties is significant, affecting not only the physical assets but also the potential social and economic benefits they could provide. As the jurisprudence around waqf continues to evolve through landmark judgments, there is a pressing need for reforms to streamline the dispute resolution process and ensure the effective management of waqf properties in line with their intended charitable purposes.

**References:**


1.	https://www.randwickresearch.com/index.php/rissj/article/download/247/204

2.	https://pib.gov.in/PressNoteDetails.aspx?NoteId=152139&ModuleId=3

3.	https://www.dailyexcelsior.com/tribunal-for-waqf-properties/

4.	https://www.drishtijudiciary.com/current-affairs/government-to-determine-waqf-properties-under-dispute

5.	https://timesofindia.indiatimes.com/india/govt-mulls-review-of-provisions-in-view-of-large-scale-litigation-over-waqf-properties/articleshow/102289755.cms

6.	https://blog.ipleaders.in/bakar-ali-vs-abu-sayid-khan-1901/

7.	https://www.drishtijudiciary.com/to-the-point/ttp-muslim-law/concept-of-waqf-under-muslim-law

8.	https://economictimes.indiatimes.com/news/india/waqf-through-the-ages-how-rs-1-lakh-crore-property-owner-board-acquires-land-and-what-the-govt-aims-to-change/articleshow/112365585.cms

9.	https://blog.ipleaders.in/concept-waqf-muslim-law/

10.     https://api.sci.gov.in/
supremecourt/2013/11190/11190_2013_39_1501_2728
9_Judgement_05-Apr-2021.pdf

---

## Chapter 7: Encroachments on Waqf Properties

**Nature and Scale of Encroachments**

Waqf properties in India face significant challenges due to widespread encroachments, which have become a major concern for the Muslim community and authorities alike. The scale of these encroachments is substantial, with government data indicating that at least 58,889 waqf properties are currently encroached upon, while more than 13,000 are embroiled in legal disputes. This alarming situation highlights the urgent need for effective measures to protect and reclaim these properties.

The nature of encroachments on waqf properties is diverse and complex. These encroachments can be broadly categorized into several types:

1. Illegal Occupation: Many waqf properties have been illegally occupied by individuals or groups who have no legal right to the land. This often occurs due to the lack of proper documentation or weak enforcement of property rights.

2. Unauthorized Construction: In some cases, encroachers have constructed buildings or structures on waqf land without permission, making it difficult to reclaim the property.

3. Government Encroachments: Surprisingly, a significant number of encroachments are by government entities themselves. The Sachar Committee report highlighted that state agencies, which are supposed to safeguard waqf interests, are often responsible for unauthorized occupation of waqf land.

4. Misuse by Caretakers: In some instances, the appointed caretakers or mutawallis of waqf properties have misused their positions, either by personally occupying the land or colluding with encroachers.

5. Disputed Ownership: Due to historical reasons and lack of proper documentation, some waqf properties face ownership disputes, leading to encroachments by parties claiming rights to the land.

The scale of the problem is further illustrated by recent government data. As of December 2024, a total of 994 waqf properties have been reported as alienated — or illegally encroached upon — across the country. Tamil Nadu alone accounts for a staggering 734 such properties, indicating a particularly severe problem in that state.

The total number of waqf properties in India is substantial, with 872,352 immovable and 16,713 movable waqf properties registered under the Waqf Act. This vast number of properties, combined with the high rate of encroachment, presents a significant challenge for management and protection.

The financial implications of these encroachments are enormous. The Sachar Committee estimated that proper management of waqf land could yield an annual income of about 120 billion rupees (approximately $1.4 billion), whereas current revenues are estimated at around 2 billion rupees. This massive discrepancy underscores the potential economic impact of reclaiming and properly managing waqf properties.

## Legal Provisions to Combat Encroachments

To address the issue of encroachments on waqf properties, several legal provisions have been put in place. The primary legislation governing waqf properties in India is the Waqf Act, 1995, which has been amended over the years to strengthen protections against encroachments.

### Key legal provisions include:

1. Section 32 of the Waqf Act: This section vests the general superintendence of all waqf properties in a state with the State Waqf Board (SWB). The SWB is empowered to manage waqf

properties, providing a legal framework for their protection.

2. Sections 54 and 55 of the Waqf Act: These sections empower the Chief Executive Officer of the State Waqf Board to take legal action against unauthorized occupation and encroachment of waqf properties. This provision is crucial for initiating legal proceedings against encroachers.

3. Waqf (Amendment) Act, 2013: This amendment strengthened the powers of waqf boards to combat encroachments. However, it has been criticized for inefficacy in addressing issues like encroachment, mismanagement, ownership disputes, and delays in registration and surveys.

4. Proposed Waqf (Amendment) Bill 2024: The central government has proposed further amendments to address ongoing challenges. However, these proposed changes have sparked debate, with some Muslim groups expressing concerns about potential negative impacts on waqf property rights.

Despite these legal provisions, enforcement remains a significant challenge. The high number of pending cases in Waqf Tribunals — 40,951 as of recent data — indicates the complexity and slow pace of legal resolution for waqf-related disputes.

## Role of State and Local Authorities

State and local authorities play a crucial role in protecting waqf properties and combating encroachments. Their responsibilities include:

1. State Waqf Boards: These boards are the primary bodies responsible for managing and protecting waqf properties at the state level. They are empowered to take legal action against encroachments and unauthorized occupations.

2. Local Revenue Authorities: These authorities are essential for maintaining accurate land records and assisting in the identification and registration of waqf properties.

3. Survey Commissioners: Appointed to conduct surveys of waqf properties, these officials play a vital role in identifying and documenting waqf lands.

4. State Governments: They are responsible for constituting waqf boards and providing necessary support for their functioning.

5. Central Waqf Council: This statutory body advises the central government on matters concerning the management and administration of waqf properties across the country. It also supervises and regulates the working of State Waqf Boards.

To improve the management and protection of waqf properties, the Ministry of Minority Affairs implements the Qaumi Waqf Board Taraqqiati Scheme (QWBTS). This scheme provides financial assistance to State Waqf Boards for various purposes, including:

- Computerization and digitization of waqf property records
- GIS mapping of waqf properties
- Maintenance of a Centralized Computing Facility
- Implementation of Enterprise Resource Planning (ERP) solutions
- Deployment of specialized manpower for better administration

As of recent data, records of 8, 02,538 immovable waqf properties have been entered in the WAMSI (Waqf Assets Management System of India) Registration Module, and GIS mapping of 2,54,533 waqf properties has been completed. These efforts aim to improve transparency and efficiency in waqf property management.

**Case Studies of Successful Reclamation**

While encroachments on waqf properties remain a significant challenge, there have been instances of successful reclamation.

These cases provide valuable insights into effective strategies for protecting and recovering waqf lands:

1. Nashik Dargah Trust Case:

The case of Shaikh Mulla Wali's Dargah in Nashik, Maharashtra, illustrates both the challenges and potential for reclaiming waqf property. The dargah trust has been engaged in a legal battle to reclaim 53 acres of land with an estimated commercial value of over Rs 2,000 crore.

Key aspects of this case include:

- The land was allegedly transferred and sold illegally.
- The trust initiated legal proceedings upon discovering the waqf status of the land in 2004.
- The case reached the Supreme Court, which directed the Maharashtra Waqf Board to report on the property's waqf status.
- The government's decision to suspend a former Waqf Board CEO who had denied the dargah's claim over the land has been seen as a positive step towards reclamation.

This case highlights the importance of legal action, persistence, and government support in reclaiming encroached waqf properties.

2. Telangana Waqf Board's Efforts:

The Telangana Waqf Board has been actively working to reclaim encroached waqf lands. As of 2024, the board is fighting 3,500 cases to reclaim approximately 55,000 acres of land.

Notable aspects of their efforts include:

- Writing letters to collectors to mutate waqf land parcels and stop registering waqf land to others since 2015.
- Dealing with complex cases, such as the 1,950 acres

> in Manikonda that were handed over to APIIC and subsequently auctioned to several companies.
> - Relying on historical documents like 'muntakhabs' (certificates of grant) by the Nizam to prove waqf status.

The Telangana case demonstrates the importance of persistent legal action and the use of historical documentation in reclaiming waqf properties.

3. Karnataka's Waqf Land Reclamation:

Karnataka has seen efforts to reclaim misused waqf properties under the Waqf Act. While specific details of successful reclamations are not provided in the search results, the state's approach includes:

- Labeling certain properties as "misused" waqf properties under the Waqf Act.
- Successive governments attempting to reclaim these lands.
- Dealing with political tensions arising from the discovery that non-Muslims and influential figures, including some Muslim leaders, had occupied portions of waqf land.

This case highlights the political complexities often involved in waqf property reclamation efforts.

These case studies underscore several key factors in successful waqf property reclamation:

1. Legal Action: Persistent legal efforts, often reaching higher courts, are crucial in challenging encroachments.

2. Documentation: Maintaining and utilizing historical records and proper documentation of waqf status is vital in proving claims.

3. Government Support: Cooperation from state authorities and

proactive measures by waqf boards are essential for effective reclamation.

4. Public Awareness: Increasing awareness about waqf properties and their importance can help in identifying and reporting encroachments.

5. Technological Solutions: Utilizing modern technologies like GIS mapping and digitization of records can aid in better management and protection of waqf properties.

6. Addressing Political Sensitivities: Given the often politically charged nature of waqf property disputes, navigating these sensitivities is crucial for successful reclamation.

In conclusion, while the encroachment of waqf properties remains a significant challenge in India, these case studies demonstrate that with persistent legal action, proper documentation, and support from authorities, it is possible to reclaim and protect these valuable assets. The ongoing efforts of various state waqf boards and the central government's initiatives to strengthen waqf management systems offer hope for more effective protection and reclamation of waqf properties in the future.

**References:**


1. https://pib.gov.in/PressNoteDetails.aspx?NoteId=152139&ModuleId=3&s=09
2. https://www.hindustantimes.com/india-news/994-waqf-properties-illegally-encroached-upon-govt-tells-parl-101733771317465.html
3. https://www.bbc.com/news/articles/c704d73kjpwo
4. https://www.pib.gov.in/PressReleasePage.aspx?PRID=1796194
5. https://pib.gov.in/PressReleasePage.aspx?PRID=1814460
6. https://blog.ipleaders.in/central-waqf-council/
7. https://indianexpress.com/article/india/nashik-dargah-

trust-in-legal-battle-to-reclaim-waqf-property-worth-rs-2000-crore-4564512/

8.	https://timesofindia.indiatimes.com/city/bengaluru/karnataka-waqf-conundrum-origins-and-current-controversy/articleshow/114970636.cms

9.	https://www.minorityaffairs.gov.in/showfile.php?lang=1&level=2&ls_id=347&lid=280

10.	https://timesofindia.indiatimes.com/city/hyderabad/telangana-waqf-board-fights-3500-cases-to-reclaim-55k-acre-land/articleshow/115652810.cms

# *Chapter 8: Socio-Economic Role of Waqf in India*

Waqf, an Islamic endowment system, has played a significant role in the socio-economic development of Muslim communities in India for centuries. This chapter explores the multifaceted contributions of waqf institutions in various sectors, including education, healthcare, housing, and community development.

## Contribution to Education

The waqf system has been instrumental in promoting education within the Muslim community in India. Historically, waqf properties have funded numerous educational institutions, from primary schools to universities, providing accessible education to countless students.

## Higher Education Institutions

One of the most notable contributions of waqf to education in India is the establishment and support of higher education institutions. For instance, Aligarh Muslim University and Jamia Millia Islamia, two prominent universities serving over 30,000 and 20,000 students respectively, have benefited significantly from waqf support. These institutions have played a crucial role in advancing education among Muslims and other communities in India.

## Primary and Secondary Education

Waqf properties have also been instrumental in supporting primary and secondary education. In Bangladesh, which shares historical and cultural ties with India, more than 8,000 educational institutions are waqf-based. This model has been replicated in various parts of India, where waqf-supported schools provide education to underprivileged communities.

## Scholarships and Financial Aid

Many waqf institutions in India provide scholarships and financial aid to students, enabling them to pursue higher education. These initiatives have been particularly beneficial for students from economically disadvantaged backgrounds, helping to bridge the educational gap within the community.

## Libraries and Research Centers

Waqf endowments have also contributed to the establishment of libraries and research centers. These facilities provide valuable resources for students and researchers, fostering a culture of learning and academic excellence within the community.

## Health Services Supported by Waqf

Waqf institutions have made significant contributions to healthcare services in India, providing accessible medical care to underserved populations.

### Hospitals and Clinics

According to the Central Waqf Council, waqf properties support over 200 hospitals and dispensaries across India. These healthcare facilities often operate on a non-profit basis, ensuring that medical services are accessible to those who cannot afford them otherwise. This contribution is particularly crucial in rural and economically disadvantaged areas where government healthcare infrastructure may be lacking.

### Specialized Medical Care

Some waqf-supported hospitals provide specialized medical care. For instance, the Shishli Children's Hospital in Istanbul, founded in 1898, serves as an example of how waqf revenues have been used to construct hospitals and support medical services, including spending on physicians, apprentices, patients, and medicines. Similar models have been adopted in India, with waqf-supported hospitals focusing on specific areas of healthcare.

## Mobile Medical Units

In addition to static healthcare facilities, some waqf institutions in India have invested in mobile medical units. These units provide essential healthcare services to remote and underserved areas, significantly improving access to medical care for rural populations.

## Medical Education and Research

Waqf institutions have also contributed to medical education and research. By supporting medical colleges and research facilities, these institutions have played a role in advancing medical knowledge and training healthcare professionals.

## Housing and Shelter for the Poor

Waqf properties have been utilized to provide housing and shelter for the poor and homeless, addressing one of the most pressing needs in many Indian communities.

## Affordable Housing Projects

Some waqf institutions have initiated affordable housing projects, providing low-cost housing options for economically disadvantaged families. These projects not only provide shelter but also contribute to the overall development of communities.

## Shelters for the Homeless

Waqf properties fund over 2,000 orphanages and shelters nationwide, according to the Ministry of Minority Affairs. These facilities provide essential services to vulnerable groups, including orphans, the elderly, and the homeless.

## Maintenance and Renovation of Existing Properties

Many waqf boards in India are involved in the maintenance and renovation of existing waqf properties to ensure they remain habitable and serve their intended purpose of providing shelter to those in need.

## Emergency Housing

During times of natural disasters or other emergencies, waqf properties have been utilized to provide temporary shelter to displaced individuals and families, demonstrating the flexibility and responsiveness of the waqf system to community needs.

## Waqf's Role in Community Development

Beyond education, healthcare, and housing, waqf institutions play a crucial role in overall community development through various initiatives.

## Infrastructure Development

Waqf properties have funded infrastructure projects such as roads, bridges, and water supply systems. For example, waqf properties in the state of Karnataka have financed the construction and maintenance of over 300 kilometers of rural roads and multiple water supply projects, enhancing the quality of life for entire communities.

## Economic Empowerment

Waqf institutions contribute to economic empowerment by providing interest-free loans to aspiring entrepreneurs, enabling them to break free from the cycle of poverty. This financial support helps in creating job opportunities and fostering economic growth within the community.

## Social Welfare Programs

Many waqf institutions run social welfare programs, including food banks, public kitchens, and support services for the elderly and disabled. These programs provide essential support to vulnerable members of the community.

## Cultural Preservation

Waqf properties often include historical and cultural sites, mosques, and madrasas. By maintaining these properties, waqf institutions play a crucial role in preserving the cultural heritage of Muslim communities in India.

## Environmental Initiatives

Some modern waqf institutions have begun to focus on environmental conservation and sustainable development. These initiatives include funding for renewable energy projects, urban green spaces, and environmental education programs.

## Promotion of Social Cohesion

By supporting various community services and bringing people together for common causes, waqf institutions promote social cohesion and a sense of community among diverse groups.

In conclusion, the socio-economic role of waqf in India is multifaceted and far-reaching. From education and healthcare to housing and community development, waqf institutions have been instrumental in addressing critical needs within Muslim communities and beyond. The potential of waqf as a tool for sustainable development and social welfare is immense, and with proper management and modernization, it can continue to play a vital role in shaping the future of Indian society.

As India faces challenges of economic disparities and social inequalities, the waqf system offers a time-tested model for community-driven development. By revitalizing and effectively managing waqf properties, there is an opportunity to create a more equitable and prosperous society, not just for the Muslim community but for all Indians. The success stories of waqf-supported institutions across various sectors demonstrate the enduring relevance and potential of this Islamic endowment system in addressing contemporary socio-economic challenges.

## References:

1.	https://www.shakebaumar.com/post/the-role-of-waqfs-in-societal-wellbeing-a-call-to-preserve-indian-waqf-properties
2.	https://digitalcommons.unl.edu/cgi/viewcontent.cgi?article=10987&context=libphilprac
3.	https://mpra.ub.uni-muenchen.de/91413/1/MPRA_paper_91413.pdf
4.	https://maktoobmedia.com/opinion/waqf-instrument-of-poverty-elimination-and-development/
5.	https://pmc.ncbi.nlm.nih.gov/articles/PMC7567918/
6.	https://forum.albaraka.site/role-of-waqf-in-socio-economic-development/?lang=en
7.	https://www.cribfb.com/journal/index.php/IJSWR/article/view/2170
8.	https://muslimmirror.com/role-of-waqf-in-the-promotion-of-higher-education-in-india/

## *Chapter 9: Women and Waqf: A Comprehensive Analysis*

The role of women in the Islamic institution of waqf (endowment) has been significant throughout history, yet often overlooked. This chapter explores the multifaceted relationship between women and waqf, examining their roles as beneficiaries, administrators, and founders, while also addressing gender disparities and highlighting specific initiatives.

### Women as Beneficiaries of Waqf

Waqf, as a charitable endowment in Islamic law, has historically played a crucial role in providing for the welfare of women. The institution of waqf has been instrumental in addressing the needs of various segments of society, including women who often faced economic vulnerabilities.

**Types of Waqf Benefiting Women**: Several categories of waqf have specifically targeted women as beneficiaries:

1. Waqf for Marriage: Historically, there have been endowments dedicated to facilitating the marriage of poor girls. For instance, Ibn Battutah reported finding waqfs in Tunis and Syria specifically established for this purpose.

2. Waqf for Divorced and Widowed Women: Some waqfs were created to provide maintenance and support for divorced women and widows. This was particularly important in societies where women might face economic hardship after the dissolution of marriage or the death of a spouse.

3. Waqf for Education: While not exclusively for women, many waqfs supported educational institutions that benefited both genders, contributing to the intellectual empowerment of women.

4. Waqf for Basic Needs: Some early examples of waqf by prominent Muslim women addressed fundamental needs. For instance, Umm al-Muminin ʿAishah and Umm al-Muminin Ṣafiyyah endowed houses for the residence of homeless persons.

## Impact on Women's Economic Security

The institution of waqf has served as a source of economic empowerment for women. By providing resources for basic needs, education, and even entrepreneurship, waqfs have historically offered a safety net for women who might otherwise face financial insecurity.

Shaista Ambar, founder of the All India Muslim Women Personal Law Board, emphasized the potential of waqf to support women and children. She stated, "People do not know it, but, Waqf is to be used for divorced women, orphaned children and destitute". This underscores the ongoing relevance of waqf as a mechanism for supporting vulnerable women in contemporary society.

## Female Involvement in Waqf Administration

While often overlooked, women have played significant roles in the administration of waqf throughout Islamic history. Their involvement ranges from founding waqfs to managing them, demonstrating women's agency in this important religious and social institution.

## Historical Perspective

The involvement of women in waqf administration can be traced back to the early days of Islam. Examples of women supervising and managing waqfs are found as early as Islam's exemplary century (khayr al-qurūn). This early participation set a precedent for women's continued involvement in waqf affairs throughout Islamic history.

## Women as Founders of Waqf

Women have been active creators of waqfs, contributing

significantly to the growth and diversity of these endowments. Historical records show that women from various social strata established waqfs for a wide range of purposes:

1. Religious Purposes: Women created waqfs for mosques, religious schools, and other institutions promoting Islamic education and practice.

2. Social Welfare: Many women-founded waqfs were dedicated to supporting the poor, orphans, and other vulnerable members of society.

3. Education: Female founders often prioritized educational institutions, contributing to the intellectual development of their communities.

4. Healthcare: Some women established waqfs for hospitals and medical facilities, addressing critical health needs.

The composition and objectives of women's waqfs reflected both continuity with traditional practices and changes in response to evolving societal needs.

## Women as Mutawallis (Administrators)

The role of women as mutawallis (administrators) of waqfs is well-documented in Islamic legal and historical sources. The Privy Council, in the case of Shahar Bano vs Aga Mohammad, held that there is no legal restriction on a woman becoming a mutawalli if the duties of the waqf do not involve religious activities. This ruling underscores the acceptance of women in administrative roles within the waqf system.

However, it's important to note that when religious duties are a part of the waqf, traditional interpretations have often excluded women from serving as mutawallis. This limitation reflects broader gender-based restrictions in certain religious contexts.

## Contemporary Efforts to Increase Women's Participation

Recent legislative efforts have aimed to increase women's representation in waqf administration. For instance, proposed amendments to the Waqf Act in India seek to mandate the inclusion of two women as members in both the Central Waqf Council and state waqf boards. This move reflects a growing recognition of the need for gender diversity in waqf governance structures.

## Gender Disparities in Waqf Distribution

Despite the historical involvement of women in waqf, gender disparities have persisted in various aspects of waqf distribution and management. These disparities reflect broader societal inequalities and have implications for the economic and social empowerment of women.

## Unequal Distribution of Benefits

Historically, the distribution of waqf benefits has often favored male beneficiaries over females. This disparity is rooted in traditional interpretations of Islamic inheritance laws, which typically allocate a larger share to male heirs. However, it's important to note that some waqf founders have used the institution to circumvent these norms and provide more equitably for female family members.

## Power Imbalances in Waqf Creation

The ability to create substantial waqfs has often been linked to economic power, which historically has been concentrated in male hands. As noted by researchers, "In the realm of economics, the disparity in power was reflected in the waqfs made by the men and women of the Mamluk elite. Although some women could use their wealth to establish significant endowments, their waqfs were generally smaller in scale compared to those of their male counterparts".

## Challenges in Administration

While women have served as mutawallis, they have often faced challenges in this role, particularly when the waqf involved religious duties. Traditional interpretations have sometimes excluded women from administering waqfs with religious components, limiting their influence in this sphere.

**Efforts to Address Disparities:** Recent initiatives aim to address these gender disparities:

1. Legislative Changes: Proposed amendments to waqf laws in some countries seek to ensure women's representation on waqf boards.

2. Awareness Campaigns: There are efforts to educate communities about the historical role of women in waqf and the importance of gender equity in waqf distribution.

3. Women-Specific Waqfs: Some contemporary waqf initiatives specifically target women's empowerment, aiming to counterbalance historical inequities.

## Case Studies of Women-Specific Waqf Initiatives

Throughout Islamic history and in contemporary times, there have been notable examples of waqf initiatives specifically designed to benefit women. These case studies illustrate the potential of waqf as a tool for women's empowerment and social development.

## Historical Case Study: Zubayr ibn al-ʿAwwam's Waqf

One of the earliest recorded instances of a waqf specifically benefiting women comes from the actions of Zubayr ibn al-ʿAwwam, a companion of the Prophet Muhammad. He dedicated houses for his "non-accepted" (al-mardudah) daughters. This waqf ensured that these women, who might otherwise have been economically vulnerable, had secure housing.

## Ottoman Era: Women's Entrepreneurship through Waqf

During the Ottoman period, women actively participated in the waqf system, both as founders and beneficiaries. Many women used waqf to support economic activities that benefited other women. For instance, some waqfs provided capital for women to start small businesses or engage in trade, fostering economic independence.

## Contemporary Case Study: Skill Development Initiatives

Shaista Ambar, advocating for the role of waqf in supporting women, suggested that "Boards should set up training centres for skill development, give out their land for small-scale enterprises so that women and their children can earn their livelihood with dignity". This proposal represents a modern approach to using waqf resources for women's economic empowerment.

## The All India Muslim Women Personal Law Board Initiative

The All India Muslim Women Personal Law Board has been advocating for more equal rights for women in marriage, including the use of waqf resources. In 2022, they approached the Supreme Court to annul unilateral talaqs (divorces), highlighting the potential role of waqf in supporting divorced women.

## Waqf for Women's Education

Many contemporary waqf initiatives focus on women's education. For example, in various Muslim-majority countries, waqf-funded scholarships and educational institutions specifically target female students, aiming to bridge the gender gap in education.

## Healthcare Waqfs for Women

Some modern waqfs have been established to address women's health issues. These include endowments for women's hospitals, maternal health clinics, and research into women's health concerns.

## Challenges and Future Directions

While the relationship between women and waqf has been significant and multifaceted, several challenges persist, and new opportunities are emerging for enhancing women's participation and benefits from the waqf system.

## Challenges

1. Legal and Cultural Barriers: In some contexts, legal frameworks and cultural norms continue to limit women's full participation in waqf administration and their access to waqf benefits.

2. Lack of Awareness: Many women, particularly in disadvantaged communities, may be unaware of their rights and potential benefits from waqf institutions.

3. Economic Disparities: The ability to create substantial waqfs often correlates with economic power, which continues to be unevenly distributed along gender lines in many societies.

4. Mismanagement and Lack of Transparency: Issues of mismanagement in some waqf institutions have led to reduced benefits for all stakeholders, including women.

## Future Directions

1. Legal Reforms: Continued efforts to reform waqf laws to ensure gender equity in representation and distribution of benefits are crucial. The proposed amendments to include women in waqf boards in India represent a step in this direction.

2. Education and Awareness: Initiatives to educate both women and men about the historical and potential role of women in waqf can help change perceptions and increase women's participation.

3. Economic Empowerment: Utilizing waqf resources for

women's economic empowerment through skill development, entrepreneurship support, and education can have far-reaching impacts.

4. Research and Documentation: More comprehensive research into women's historical and contemporary roles in waqf can provide insights for policy-making and inspire greater involvement.

5. Technology and Transparency: Leveraging technology for better management and transparency in waqf administration can benefit all stakeholders, including women.

6. Innovative Waqf Models: Developing new models of waqf that specifically address contemporary women's issues, such as workplace equality, childcare support, and protection from domestic violence.

In conclusion, the relationship between women and waqf is rich and complex, reflecting both the challenges and opportunities present in broader societal structures. By addressing existing disparities and leveraging the potential of waqf for women's empowerment, this Islamic institution can continue to play a vital role in promoting gender equity and social development in Muslim societies and beyond.

**References**


1.      Ambar, S. (2024). Waqf should step in to provide maintenance to women and children. The Week. https://www.theweek.in/news/india/2024/07/11/waqf-should-step-in-to-provide-maintenance-to-women-and-children-shaista-ambar.html

2.      Fay, M. A. (2018). The Role of Women in the Creation and Management of Awqāf. Intellectual Discourse, Special Issue, 1036-1037.

3.      Government of India. (2024). Proposed bill seeks to make

women waqf board members. Times of India. https://timesofindia.indiatimes.com/india/proposed-bill-seeks-to-make-women-waqf-board-members/articleshow/112270799.cms

4.   Humphreys, R. S. (1994). Women and Gender in Medieval Islamic Societies: A Bibliographic Essay. In Women as Patrons of Architecture in Ayyubid Damascus (pp. 35-37).

5.   Lawctopus. (n.d.). Concept Of Waqf Under Muslim Law. Academike. https://www.lawctopus.com/academike/concept-waqf-muslim-law/

6.   Ministry of Minority Affairs, Government of India. (2024). Waqf Act Amendments: Tighter control, more women and non-Muslims members. Economic Times. https://economictimes.indiatimes.com/news/india/waqf-act-amendments-tighter-control-more-women-and-non-muslims-members-five-key-changes-to-waqf-law/articleshow/112373521.cms

7.   Sato, T. (2019). A Testamentary Waqf and Its Female Founder/Administrator in Late Fourteenth-Century Egypt. Orient, 54, 41-42.

# Chapter 10: Challenges in Waqf Administration

The administration of Waqf properties, despite their immense potential for socio-economic development, faces numerous challenges that hinder their effective management and utilization. This chapter delves into four critical areas of concern: lack of accountability and transparency, insufficient financial management, bureaucratic hurdles, and political interference and mismanagement.

## Lack of Accountability and Transparency

One of the most pressing issues in Waqf administration is the glaring lack of accountability and transparency. This deficiency has led to widespread mismanagement and underutilization of Waqf assets, significantly impacting the Muslim community's welfare.

## Ineffective Oversight

The current system of Waqf management often lacks robust oversight mechanisms. Many Waqf boards operate with minimal external scrutiny, leading to a lack of accountability in their operations. This absence of effective checks and balances has created an environment where misuse of Waqf properties and funds can occur unchecked.

## Opaque Financial Reporting

Financial reporting in Waqf administration is often opaque and inconsistent. Many Waqf boards fail to maintain proper accounts of properties and their revenues, making it difficult to track the utilization of funds and assets. This lack of transparency not only hampers efficient management but also erodes public trust in the Waqf system.

## Limited Public Access to Information

The lack of transparency extends to limited public access to information about Waqf properties and their management. This opacity prevents stakeholders, including beneficiaries and potential donors, from understanding how Waqf assets are being utilized and managed. Consequently, this lack of information discourages community participation and oversight in Waqf affairs.

**Inadequate Performance Measurement**

Many Waqf institutions lack comprehensive performance measurement systems. Without clear metrics to evaluate the effectiveness of Waqf management, it becomes challenging to hold administrators accountable for their decisions and actions. This absence of performance evaluation contributes to the perpetuation of inefficient practices.

**Misuse of Waqf Properties**

The lack of accountability has led to instances of misuse and even illegal appropriation of Waqf properties. Some influential individuals have been known to hinder the growth of Awqaf and seize their funds for personal gain. This misuse not only depletes Waqf resources but also diverts them from their intended charitable purposes.

**Recommendations for Improvement:** To address these accountability and transparency issues, several measures can be implemented:

1. Implementation of Digital Systems: Adopting blockchain technology or other digital record-keeping systems can enhance transparency and traceability in Waqf management.

2. Regular Audits: Conducting regular, independent audits of Waqf boards and properties can help identify and address irregularities.

3. Public Reporting: Implementing mandatory public reporting

of Waqf finances and activities can increase transparency and public trust.

4. Stakeholder Engagement: Involving community members and beneficiaries in Waqf management decisions can improve accountability and ensure that Waqf assets are used for their intended purposes.

5. Performance Metrics: Developing and implementing clear performance metrics for Waqf management can help in evaluating the effectiveness of administrators and identifying areas for improvement.

## Insufficient Financial Management

The financial management of Waqf properties is another area fraught with challenges. Despite the vast potential for generating substantial revenues, many Waqf properties are underutilized or mismanaged, resulting in significant financial losses.

## Outdated Rental Structures

One of the most glaring issues in Waqf financial management is the outdated rental structure for Waqf-owned properties. Many of these properties are leased at rates that were set decades ago, some dating back to the 1950s. This archaic pricing model results in absurdly low rental income, far below current market rates. Even more concerning is that even these meager rents are often not collected regularly, further diminishing the potential revenue from Waqf properties.

## Underutilization of Assets

The Sachar Committee report of 2006 estimated that Waqf properties could generate an annual income of Rs 12,000 crore. However, recent surveys by the Ministry of Minority Affairs reveal that the actual number of Waqf properties exceeds 8.72 lakh, suggesting that the potential income could be as high as Rs 20,000 crore annually. Despite this enormous potential, the actual revenue generated remains a paltry Rs 200 crore—a mere fraction of what could be achieved with professional and transparent management.

## Lack of Professional Financial Management

Many Waqf boards lack professional financial management expertise. This deficiency leads to poor investment decisions, inefficient use of resources, and missed opportunities for revenue generation. The absence of strategic financial planning and modern financial management techniques significantly hampers the growth and sustainability of Waqf assets.

## Inadequate Record-Keeping

Poor record-keeping practices exacerbate the financial management challenges. Many Waqf boards fail to maintain accurate and up-to-date records of their properties, revenues, and expenditures. This lack of proper documentation makes it difficult to track financial performance, plan for the future, or make informed decisions about asset management.

## Limited Financial Transparency

The lack of financial transparency in Waqf management not only hampers accountability but also affects financial planning and decision-making. Without clear and accessible financial reports, it becomes challenging to identify areas of financial inefficiency or opportunities for improvement.

## Misallocation of Funds

In some cases, Waqf funds are not allocated according to the intended purposes specified by the donors. For instance, during the Ottoman era, a large portion of Waqf funds was spent on shrines rather than on education and other services that met people's needs. This misallocation of funds not only violates the donors' intentions but also reduces the socio-economic impact of Waqf.

**Recommendations for Improvement:** To address these financial management challenges, several measures can be implemented:

1. Market-Based Rental Revisions: Updating rental rates for Waqf properties to reflect current market values can significantly increase revenue.

2. Professional Financial Management: Hiring qualified financial professionals to manage Waqf assets can improve investment decisions and overall financial performance.

3. Modern Accounting Systems: Implementing modern accounting and financial management systems can improve record-keeping and financial transparency.

4. Strategic Financial Planning: Developing long-term financial strategies for Waqf assets can help maximize returns and ensure sustainable growth.

5. Regular Financial Audits: Conducting regular financial audits can help identify areas of inefficiency and prevent misuse of funds.

6. Diversification of Investments: Exploring diverse investment opportunities can help maximize returns on Waqf assets while managing risk.

## Bureaucratic Hurdles in Waqf Administration

The administration of Waqf properties is often hindered by bureaucratic hurdles that slow down decision-making processes, create inefficiencies, and sometimes lead to the mismanagement of Waqf assets.

## Excessive Government Control

One of the primary bureaucratic challenges in Waqf administration is the excessive control exerted by government bodies. The Waqf (Amendment) Bill 2024 has raised concerns about increased bureaucratic control, with the involvement of District Collectors and other senior government officials in Waqf management. While this aims to increase transparency, it may lead to increased bureaucratic red tape and delays.

### Slow Decision-Making Processes

The involvement of multiple government bodies in Waqf administration often results in slow decision-making processes. This bureaucratic sluggishness can lead to delays in implementing important projects, resolving disputes, and responding to changing market conditions. Such delays can significantly impact the effective management and development of Waqf properties.

### Lack of Specialized Knowledge

Government officials involved in Waqf management may not always possess the specialized knowledge required to understand the religious and cultural nuances of Waqf properties. This lack of expertise can lead to decisions that may not align with the principles and objectives of Waqf.

### Overlapping Jurisdictions

The administration of Waqf often involves multiple government departments and agencies, leading to overlapping jurisdictions and conflicting directives. This bureaucratic complexity can create confusion, delay decision-making, and hinder the efficient management of Waqf properties.

### Rigid Administrative Structures

Many Waqf boards operate under rigid administrative structures that lack flexibility and adaptability. These inflexible systems can make it difficult to implement innovative management practices or respond quickly to changing circumstances.

## Inadequate Coordination with Local Authorities

Waqf boards often face challenges in coordinating with local revenue authorities and other government departments. This lack of effective coordination can lead to issues in property registration, survey work, and addressing encroachments on Waqf lands.

**Recommendations for Improvement:** To address these bureaucratic hurdles, several measures can be implemented:

1. Streamlined Decision-Making Processes: Implementing more efficient decision-making processes within Waqf boards can help reduce bureaucratic delays.

2. Capacity Building: Providing specialized training to government officials involved in Waqf management can enhance their understanding of Waqf principles and improve decision-making.

3. Clear Demarcation of Responsibilities: Clearly defining the roles and responsibilities of different government bodies involved in Waqf administration can help reduce overlapping jurisdictions and conflicts.

4. Adoption of Technology: Implementing digital systems for Waqf management can help streamline administrative processes and reduce bureaucratic hurdles.

5. Enhanced Coordination Mechanisms: Establishing better coordination mechanisms between Waqf boards and other government departments can improve overall efficiency in Waqf administration.

6. Autonomy in Operations: Granting more operational autonomy to Waqf boards, while maintaining necessary oversight, can help reduce bureaucratic interference and improve efficiency.

## Political Interference and Mismanagement

Political interference and mismanagement have long plagued the administration of Waqf properties, often leading to the erosion of trust in the Waqf system and hampering its effectiveness in serving the Muslim community.

## Politicization of Waqf Boards

Waqf boards are often subject to political influence, with appointments to key positions sometimes based on political considerations rather than merit or expertise. This politicization can lead to decisions that serve political interests rather than the welfare of the community or the objectives of the Waqf.

## Misuse of Power

The concentration of power in Waqf boards, coupled with political influence, has sometimes led to the misuse of Waqf properties and funds. There have been instances where influential individuals have used various means to hinder the growth of Awqaf and seize their funds for personal or political gain.

## Short-Term Focus

Political interference often results in a focus on short-term gains rather than long-term development of Waqf properties. Governments may use Waqf for specific projects to achieve political gains rather than focusing on sustainable, long-term development that aligns with the Waqf's objectives.

## Erosion of Trust

The perceived political interference in Waqf affairs has led to a loss of trust in the Waqf system among the Muslim community. This erosion of trust has deterred individuals from making new Waqf endowments, fearing the state's intentions in managing Waqf revenues.

## Lack of Continuity in Management

Political changes can lead to frequent changes in Waqf board leadership and management, resulting in a lack of continuity in policies and projects. This instability can hinder the implementation of long-term strategies and development plans for Waqf properties.

## Interference in Religious Affairs

Some Muslim organizations, such as the All India Muslim Personal Law Board (AIMPLB), have raised concerns about government interference in Waqf matters, arguing that Waqf is a religious institution and should remain autonomous. This perceived intrusion into religious affairs has created tension between the government and sections of the Muslim community.

**Recommendations for Improvement:** To address the challenges of political interference and mismanagement, several measures can be implemented:

1. Merit-Based Appointments: Implementing a transparent, merit-based system for appointments to Waqf boards can help reduce political influence and ensure competent management.

2. Independent Oversight: Establishing independent oversight committees that include community representatives can help prevent misuse of power and ensure adherence to Waqf objectives.

3. Long-Term Strategic Planning: Developing and adhering to long-term strategic plans for Waqf development can help mitigate the impact of short-term political considerations.

4. Transparency in Decision-Making: Implementing transparent decision-making processes and regular public reporting can help rebuild trust in the Waqf system.

5. Legal Safeguards: Strengthening legal safeguards against political interference and misuse of Waqf properties can help

protect the integrity of the Waqf system.

6. Community Engagement: Involving the Muslim community in Waqf management decisions can help ensure that Waqf properties are used in line with community needs and religious principles.

In conclusion, addressing the challenges of lack of accountability and transparency, insufficient financial management, bureaucratic hurdles, and political interference in Waqf administration requires a multi-faceted approach. By implementing comprehensive reforms that focus on transparency, professionalism, efficiency, and community engagement, the Waqf system can be revitalized to fulfill its potential as a powerful tool for the socio-economic development of the Muslim community. The recent legislative efforts, such as the Waqf (Amendment) Bill 2024, represent steps in the right direction, but their success will depend on effective implementation and continued commitment to reform from all stakeholders involved in Waqf administration.

**References:**


1. https://doonlawmentor.com/waqf-amendment-bill-2024-a-bold-reform-or-government-overreach/
2. https://pib.gov.in/PressNoteDetails.aspx?NoteId=152139&ModuleId=3 https://guides.libraries.psu.edu/apaquickguide/intext
3. https://www.scribbr.com/apa-style/in-text-citation/
4. https://orca.cardiff.ac.uk/id/eprint/46875/8/2013%20siraj%20siti.pdf
5. https://ibwaqf.org.uk/news/blog/waqf-management-problems
6. https://owl.purdue.edu/owl/research_and_citation/apa_style/apa_formatting_and_style_guide/in_text_citations_the_basics.html
7. https://www.financialexpress.com/opinion/reforming-

waqf-a-call-for-transparent-and-accountable-management-for-the-welfare-of-the-muslim-community/3580685/

8.      https://www.milligazette.com/news/6-issues/34121-challenges-around-waqf-in-india/

9.                          https://www.researchgate.net/publication/366695348_ADDRESSING_ACCOUNTABILITY_AND_TRANSPARENCY_CHALLENGES_IN_WAQF_MANAGEMENT_USING_BLOCKCHAIN_TECHNOLOGY

## *Chapter 11: Waqf and Urbanization in India*

The intersection of waqf properties and urban development in India presents a complex landscape of challenges and opportunities. As cities expand and modernize, waqf lands—properties dedicated for religious or charitable purposes under Islamic law—face increasing pressure from urbanization. This chapter explores the multifaceted relationship between waqf and urban development in India, examining the impacts, conflicts, and potential for transformation.

**Impact of Urban Development on Waqf Properties**

Urban development has significantly affected waqf properties across India, often in ways that challenge their traditional roles and management. As cities grow, waqf lands that were once on the periphery find themselves in prime urban locations, subject to new pressures and opportunities.

**Encroachment and Displacement**

One of the most pressing issues facing waqf properties in urban areas is encroachment. In 2019, it was reported that approximately 17,000 waqf properties had been encroached upon across the country. This widespread encroachment not only diminishes the physical space available for waqf purposes but also erodes the potential benefits these properties could provide to the Muslim community and society at large.

The rapid pace of urban development has led to instances where long-standing communities on waqf lands face displacement. In Kerala's coastal area of Munambam, for example, residents who have lived on the land for nearly 30 years are under pressure due to recent notifications claiming their properties as waqf land. This situation highlights the tension between historical land use and modern legal classifications.

## Economic Pressures and Opportunities

Urbanization has dramatically increased the value of many waqf properties, particularly those in central urban locations. However, this increase in value has not always translated into benefits for the waqf institutions or the communities they serve. Many waqf properties are rented out at rates fixed decades ago, sometimes as far back as the 1950s. This outdated rental structure severely limits the revenue potential of these properties.

The Sachar Committee report of 2006 estimated that waqf properties could generate an annual income of Rs 12,000 crore. More recent surveys suggest that with over 8.72 lakh waqf properties now identified, the potential income could be as high as Rs 20,000 crore annually. However, the actual revenue generated remains a mere fraction of this potential, at around Rs 200 crore.

## Environmental and Infrastructure Challenges

Urban development has also brought environmental and infrastructure challenges to waqf properties. In some areas, rapid construction has led to issues such as flooding and poor ventilation for residents on waqf lands. For instance, in certain waqf areas, even moderate rainfall can lead to flooding due to inadequate drainage systems and the impact of nearby hill development.

## Transforming Waqf Properties into Urban Assets

Despite the challenges, there is significant potential for transforming waqf properties into valuable urban assets that can benefit both the Muslim community and the broader urban fabric.

## Development Initiatives

The Indian government has recognized the potential of

waqf properties and has initiated schemes to promote their development. The Shahari Waqf Sampatti Vikas Yojana launched in 1974-75 and recently extended until 2025-26, aims to provide loan assistance for developing economically viable projects on waqf lands. This scheme supports the construction of commercial arcades, marriage halls, hospitals, and other revenue-generating structures on waqf properties.

## Modernization and Revenue Generation

Modernizing waqf properties can significantly enhance their revenue-generating potential. For example, properties on MI Road in Jaipur, currently rented out for as little as Rs 300 per month, could potentially fetch up to Rs 25,000 per month if rent policies are updated. Such increases in revenue could fund the establishment of world-class institutions—schools, universities, and hospitals—that serve not only the Muslim community but society at large.

## Innovative Use of Urban Waqf Properties

Some waqf boards and institutions are exploring innovative ways to utilize urban waqf properties. These include developing mixed-use complexes that combine commercial spaces with community facilities, creating educational hubs, and establishing healthcare centers. Such developments can provide sustainable income streams while fulfilling the charitable objectives of waqf institutions.

## Land Use Conflicts in Urban Areas

The urban context has given rise to various land use conflicts involving waqf properties, stemming from competing claims, legal ambiguities, and developmental pressures.

## Legal and Ownership Disputes

In many urban areas, waqf properties are subject to legal disputes and ownership conflicts. In Tamilnadu's

Thiruchendurai village, for instance, the Waqf Board has claimed vast portions of land, including private homes, Hindu temples, and areas of historical significance. Such sweeping claims have led to intense frustration among residents, as their ancestral lands and cultural sites are now being contested.

Similar issues have arisen in other states. In Karnataka, an overnight notification declared approximately 1,500 acres of land as waqf property in Vijayapura, affecting many farmers who suddenly found their agricultural lands under waqf jurisdiction.

## Urban Planning and Zoning Challenges

The integration of waqf properties into modern urban planning frameworks presents significant challenges. Many waqf properties were established long before current zoning regulations and urban master plans were conceived. As a result, their traditional uses may conflict with contemporary urban zoning requirements.

Moreover, the unique legal status of waqf properties can complicate their inclusion in urban development plans. Urban planners must navigate the delicate balance between preserving the integrity and purpose of waqf lands while accommodating the needs of growing cities.

## Community Tensions

The management and development of urban waqf properties have sometimes led to tensions between different community groups. In some cases, non-Muslim communities living on or near waqf lands have expressed concerns about potential displacement or changes in land use that could affect their livelihoods or cultural practices.

## Role of Urban Planning in Protecting Waqf

Urban planning plays a crucial role in protecting waqf properties while integrating them into the broader urban fabric. Effective urban planning can help resolve conflicts, preserve the integrity of waqf institutions, and maximize the benefits of these properties for both the Muslim community and the wider urban population.

**Inclusive Urban Planning Approaches:** Urban planners need to adopt inclusive approaches that recognize the unique status and potential of waqf properties. This involves:

1. Comprehensive Surveys: Conducting thorough surveys of waqf properties within urban areas to accurately map their extent and current use.

2. Stakeholder Engagement: Involving waqf boards, local communities, and urban development authorities in collaborative planning processes.

3. Adaptive Reuse Strategies: Developing strategies for the adaptive reuse of waqf properties that respect their original purpose while meeting contemporary urban needs.

**Legal and Policy Frameworks:** Strengthening legal and policy frameworks is essential for protecting waqf properties in urban contexts. This includes:

1. Clear Demarcation: Establishing clear legal mechanisms for demarcating and registering waqf properties to prevent encroachment and resolve ownership disputes.

2. Zoning Regulations: Developing specific zoning regulations that accommodate the unique nature of waqf properties while ensuring their integration into the urban fabric.

3. Development Guidelines: Creating guidelines for the development of waqf properties that balance revenue generation with community welfare objectives.

**Capacity Building and Modernization:** Enhancing the capacity of waqf boards and institutions to manage urban properties effectively is crucial. This involves:

1. Professional Management: Introducing professional management practices in waqf administration to improve efficiency and transparency.

2. Technology Integration: Implementing digital record-keeping systems and GIS mapping for better management of waqf properties.

3. Financial Expertise: Developing financial expertise within waqf institutions to maximize the economic potential of urban waqf properties.

**Sustainable Development Models:** Urban planners can promote sustainable development models for waqf properties that serve multiple objectives:

1. Mixed-Use Development: Encouraging mixed-use developments on waqf lands that combine commercial, residential, and community spaces.

2. Green Infrastructure: Integrating waqf properties into urban green infrastructure plans, preserving open spaces and enhancing environmental quality.

3. Cultural Preservation: Incorporating heritage conservation principles in the development of historically significant waqf properties.

The intersection of waqf and urbanization in India presents both challenges and opportunities. While urban development has put pressure on waqf properties through encroachment, outdated management practices, and legal disputes, it has also created potential for these properties to become significant urban assets. The transformation of waqf properties into modern, revenue-generating entities while maintaining their charitable essence is crucial for their relevance and sustainability in urban India.

Effective urban planning, coupled with legal reforms and capacity building, can play a pivotal role in protecting waqf properties and enhancing their contribution to urban development. By adopting inclusive planning approaches, strengthening legal frameworks, and promoting sustainable development models, urban planners can help reconcile the traditional purposes of waqf with the demands of modern urbanization.

The future of waqf in urban India lies in striking a balance between preserving its religious and charitable character and adapting to the realities of contemporary urban life. With thoughtful planning and management, waqf properties can not only survive but thrive in India's rapidly urbanizing landscape, contributing significantly to both community welfare and urban development.

**References:**

1. Brader, T. (2006). Campaigning for hearts and minds: How emotional appeals in political ads work. University of Chicago Press.

2. Central Waqf Council. (n.d.). Shahari Waqf Sampatti Vikas Yojana. Retrieved from https://centralwaqfcouncil.gov.in/content/waqf-development-0

3. Denhart, H. (2008). Deconstructing barriers: Perceptions of students labeled with learning disabilities in higher education. Journal of Learning Disabilities, 41(6), 483-497. https://doi.org/10.1177/0022219408321151

4. Financial Express. (2024, August 12). Reforming Waqf: A Call for Transparent and Accountable Management for the Welfare of the Muslim Community. Retrieved from https://www.financialexpress.com/opinion/reforming-waqf-a-call-for-transparent-and-accountable-management-for-the-welfare-of-the-muslim-

community/3580685/

5.    Government of India, Ministry of Minority Affairs. (2017). Shahari Waqf Sampatti Vikas Yojana. Retrieved from https://uttarakhandwaqfboard.uk.gov.in/files/acts/SWSVY_ENG.pdf

6.    Miller, T. E., & Schuh, J. H. (2005). Promoting reasonable expectations: Aligning student and institutional views of the college experience. Jossey-Bass.

7.    Mohamad Shaharudin Bin Samsurijan. (2020). Issues and Challenges of Urban Residents in Waqf Land Area. The Online Journal of Quality in Higher Education, 7(2), 153-161.

8.    The India Forum. (2024, November 25). Wakf Reforms or a Bid to Control Waqf Properties? Retrieved from  https://www.theindiaforum.in/law/wakf-reforms-or-bid-control-waqf-properties

# Chapter 12: Economic Potential of Waqf Properties

Waqf, an Islamic endowment system, has played a significant role in the socio-economic development of Muslim societies throughout history. In recent years, there has been a growing interest in revitalizing and maximizing the economic potential of waqf properties to address contemporary challenges and contribute to sustainable development. This chapter explores the economic potential of waqf properties, focusing on their commercial utilization, investment opportunities, challenges, and successful models from various countries.

## Commercial Utilization of Waqf Properties

The commercial utilization of waqf properties represents a significant opportunity to generate sustainable income for charitable purposes while preserving the original assets. This approach aligns with the fundamental principles of waqf, which emphasize the perpetual nature of the endowment and the ongoing distribution of benefits to designated beneficiaries.

One of the primary methods of commercial utilization is the development of waqf lands into income-generating properties. This can include the construction of commercial complexes, office buildings, or residential units on waqf land. For instance, in Bengaluru, India, the state government has decided to develop waqf properties that are not under dispute for commercial purposes. This initiative aims to leverage rising real estate prices and generate revenue for the welfare of the minority community.The development of waqf properties for commercial use can take various forms:

1. Mixed-use developments: These projects combine multiple functions within a single property. An excellent example is the redevelopment of an old mosque in Singapore into a mixed complex comprising a mosque, a commercial complex,

and 103 service apartments. This approach not only preserves the religious function of the waqf but also creates additional revenue streams.

2. Public-private partnerships: Collaborations between waqf authorities and private developers can lead to mutually beneficial outcomes. In Penang, Malaysia, a state religious authority partnered with a property developer under a profit-sharing agreement to develop vacant waqf land (Wakaf Seetee Aisah) into terrace houses and shop offices. This model allows for the expertise and capital of private developers to be leveraged while ensuring that the waqf benefits from the development.

3. Leasing arrangements: Waqf properties can be leased to businesses or individuals for commercial purposes. This approach provides a steady income stream without requiring significant capital investment from the waqf institution. The Islamic Development Bank (IsDB) has established the Awqaf Properties Investment Fund (APIF), which uses leasing and istisna' for the construction of residential buildings, office/commercial buildings, and mixed-use development of waqf lands.

4. Retail and hospitality: Waqf properties in prime locations can be developed into shopping centers, hotels, or restaurants. For example, in Bangladesh, a large shopping complex in Dhaka is waqf-based, providing employment to many people and even financing a publication house, a large auditorium, and a mosque.

The commercial utilization of waqf properties not only generates income but also contributes to urban development, job creation, and economic growth. However, it is crucial to ensure that such developments adhere to Islamic principles and the original intentions of the waqf donors. As noted by Mohammad Mohsin, Secretary for haj, waqf and minority affairs in Karnataka, India, "We will have stringent conditions on the sale of pork, liquor and other things that are forbidden by the Islamic faith".

## Investment Opportunities in Waqf Land

Waqf lands present numerous investment opportunities that can enhance their economic potential while fulfilling their social and religious objectives. These opportunities range from traditional real estate development to innovative financial instruments.

1. Real estate development: Waqf lands in urban areas often have significant development potential. Investors can partner with waqf institutions to develop these lands into commercial, residential, or mixed-use properties. The National Waqf Development Corporation (Nawadco) in India is taking the lead in developing waqf properties in various states. Such developments can significantly increase the value and income-generating capacity of waqf lands.

2. Agricultural investments: For waqf lands in rural areas, agricultural investments can be a viable option. This could involve modern farming techniques, agribusiness ventures, or sustainable agriculture projects. The International Shari'ah Research Academy for Islamic Finance (ISRA) is working with the Islamic Development Bank on a project to set up and operationalize sheep and dairy farms on waqf lands.

3. Renewable energy projects: Waqf lands can be utilized for renewable energy projects such as solar farms or wind turbines. These projects not only generate income but also contribute to environmental sustainability. ISRA's collaboration with the IsDB includes plans for renewable energy projects on waqf lands.

4. Educational and healthcare facilities: Investing in the development of schools, universities, hospitals, or clinics on waqf lands can fulfill important social needs while generating income through fees or rentals. Historically, waqf has played

a significant role in funding educational institutions, as exemplified by the Süleymaniye Waqf in Istanbul, which funded the construction of schools and universities.

5. Cash waqf and financial instruments: The concept of cash waqf opens up new investment opportunities. Islamic banks and financial institutions can create investment products based on cash waqf, allowing for more flexible and diversified investment strategies. In Malaysia, several Islamic banks promote and practice cash waqf schemes.

6. Sukuk issuance: Waqf-based sukuk (Islamic bonds) represent an innovative way to raise capital for developing waqf properties. ISRA is working on issuing awqaf sukuk worth USD100 million, which will be used to finance various projects benefiting waqf beneficiaries worldwide.

7. Technology and innovation hubs: Waqf lands can be developed into technology parks or innovation centers, attracting startups and established companies. This aligns with the historical role of waqf in promoting education and innovation in Muslim societies.

8. Tourism and cultural projects: For waqf properties with historical or cultural significance, investments in tourism-related projects can be lucrative. This could include museums, cultural centers, or heritage hotels.

When considering investment opportunities in waqf land, it is essential to balance economic returns with social impact and adherence to Islamic principles. As Ahmed (2004) notes, the role of waqf extends beyond mere economic gains to encompass poverty alleviation and social development.

## Challenges in Realizing Economic Potential

Despite the significant economic potential of waqf properties, several challenges hinder their effective utilization and development. Addressing these challenges is crucial for unlocking the full economic potential of waqf assets.

1. Legal and regulatory issues: Many countries lack comprehensive and enabling regulatory frameworks for waqf management and development. In India, for example, the Waqf Act of 1954 failed to address some unlawful practices, leading to mismanagement and corruption. Developing clear, standardized, and transparent laws regarding waqf management across all regions is essential for attracting investment and ensuring proper utilization of waqf properties.

2. Encroachment and illegal occupation: One of the most significant obstacles facing the waqf system in many countries is the illegal occupation of waqf properties. As noted in the challenges facing waqf properties in India, "Many had suffered at the hands of private parties, government departments, and business entities as their Waqf properties were illegally snatched from them". This issue not only deprives waqf institutions of potential income but also complicates development efforts.

3. Mismanagement and corruption: Widespread allegations of falsification and ineptitude in the management of waqf properties by Mutawallis (waqf managers) and State Waqf Boards have been reported. This mismanagement has led to the underutilization of waqf properties and, in some cases, significant losses. Implementing professional management practices and enhancing transparency in waqf administration are crucial steps in addressing this challenge.

4. Lack of comprehensive data and records: Incomplete and outdated waqf records pose a significant challenge to effective management and development. The Waqf Amendment Act of 2013 in India mandated the digitization of waqf records to improve transparency and accountability. However, the process has been slow, and many Waqf Boards still rely on paper records, which are prone to tampering, loss, or forgery.

5. Limited financial resources: Many waqf institutions lack the financial resources necessary for developing or maintaining their properties. This limitation can lead to the deterioration of waqf assets and missed opportunities for economic development. Innovative financing mechanisms, such as sukuk issuance or partnerships with Islamic financial institutions, can help address this challenge.

6. Lack of professional expertise: The management of waqf properties often requires specialized knowledge in areas such as real estate development, finance, and investment management. Many waqf institutions lack this expertise, limiting their ability to maximize the economic potential of their assets. Training programs and partnerships with professional organizations can help build capacity within waqf institutions.

7. Balancing economic and social objectives: While realizing the economic potential of waqf properties is important, it must be balanced with the social and religious objectives of the waqf. Ensuring that commercial developments do not compromise the original intentions of the waqf donors or the needs of the beneficiaries can be challenging.

8. Political interference: In some cases, political interference in waqf management can hinder effective decision-making and development efforts. Establishing independent regulatory bodies or strengthening existing ones could help address issues of encroachment and unlawful occupation of waqf land.

9. Public awareness and acceptance: There is often a lack of public awareness about the potential of waqf properties and the importance of their development. Increasing public understanding and acceptance of commercial utilization of waqf assets is crucial for garnering support for development initiatives.

10. Environmental and social impact considerations: As waqf properties are developed, ensuring that projects are

environmentally sustainable and socially responsible can be challenging. Implementing rigorous environmental and social impact assessments for waqf development projects is essential.

Addressing these challenges requires a multi-faceted approach involving legal reforms, capacity building, technological adoption, and increased transparency in waqf management. As Kahf (2007) argues, the general idea of establishing a waqf is for the cause of humanity, and overcoming these challenges is crucial for realizing this noble objective in the contemporary context.

## Successful Models from Other Countries

Several countries have implemented successful models for realizing the economic potential of waqf properties. These models offer valuable insights and best practices that can be adapted and applied in other contexts.

1. Singapore: The Islamic Religious Council of Singapore (MUIS) has been at the forefront of innovative waqf development. One notable example is the redevelopment of an old mosque into a mixed-use complex comprising a mosque, commercial spaces, and service apartments. This model demonstrates how waqf properties can be developed to serve both religious and commercial purposes, significantly increasing their income-generating potential.

2. Malaysia: The country has implemented several successful waqf development models:

a) Cash Waqf: In 2007, Malaysia issued a national fatwa permitting cash waqf, leading to the introduction of several cash waqf schemes by local banks, Yayasan Wakaf Malaysia, and State Islamic Religious Councils. This innovation has allowed for greater flexibility in waqf investments and broader public participation.

b) Corporate Waqf: Malaysia has pioneered the concept of

corporate waqf, where companies establish waqf funds as part of their corporate social responsibility initiatives. For example, Johor Corporation established the first corporate waqf in Malaysia, which has funded various social and economic development projects.

c) Waqf Real Estate Development: The joint development of Wakaf Seetee Aisah in Penang into terrace houses and shop offices through a partnership between the state religious authority and a private developer showcases a successful public-private partnership model.

3. Turkey: The country has a rich history of waqf institutions and has implemented several successful models:

a) Vehbi Koç Foundation: This is considered one of the first documented cases of corporate waqf. The foundation focuses on education, healthcare, and culture, demonstrating how modern corporate structures can be integrated with the waqf concept.
b) Restoration and Commercialization: Turkey has successfully restored many historical waqf properties and repurposed them for commercial use, such as converting old Hans (inns) into boutique hotels or shopping centers.

4. Kuwait: The Kuwait Awqaf Public Foundation (KAPF) has implemented a strategic approach to waqf development:

a) Investment Diversification: KAPF has diversified its investments across various sectors, including real estate, financial markets, and direct investments in companies.

b) International Waqf Fund: Kuwait established an international waqf fund to support Islamic causes globally, showcasing how waqf can be used for international development and diplomacy.

5. Saudi Arabia: The country has implemented several initiatives to develop waqf properties:

a) Waqf Investment Funds: Saudi Arabia has established

specialized investment funds for waqf properties, allowing for professional management and diversification of investments.

b) Mega Projects: The development of large-scale waqf projects, such as the King Abdul Aziz Waqf in Makkah, which includes hotels, commercial centers, and residential units, demonstrates the potential for waqf to contribute to urban development.

6. Indonesia: The country has implemented innovative approaches to waqf development:

a) Productive Waqf: Indonesia has promoted the concept of "productive waqf," where waqf assets are invested in income-generating activities. For example, the Dompet Dhuafa foundation has developed waqf-based hospitals that provide free healthcare to the poor while generating income from paying patients.

b) Waqf-linked Sukuk: Indonesia has issued waqf-linked sukuk, an innovative financial instrument that allows for the development of waqf properties through Islamic capital market instruments.

These successful models demonstrate that with innovative approaches, proper management, and supportive regulatory frameworks, waqf properties can realize their full economic potential while fulfilling their social and religious objectives. As Cizakca (2011) points out, the key role of the waqf sector in providing public services can lead to significant reductions in government expenditure and borrowing, potentially reducing the tax burden on the public and increasing private investment and growth.

## References


1.  Ahmed, H. (2004). Role of Zakat and Awqaf in Poverty Alleviation. Jeddah, Saudi Arabia: Islamic Development Bank Group, Islamic Research and Training Institute.
2.  Baskan, B. (2002). Waqf System as a Redistribution

Mechanism in the Ottoman Empire. Paper presented at 17th Middle East History and Theory Conference. May 10-11.

3.     Boudjellal, M. (2008). The need for a new approach to the role in socio-economic development of waqf in the 21st century. Review of Islamic Economics, 12(2), 125-136.

4.     Brown, R. A., & Holloway, R. (2007). Islamic Philanthropy and the Evolution of Social Entrepreneurship in Southeast Asia. In Proceedings of the 4th ASEAN Inter-University Seminar on Social Development.

5.     Cajee, Z. A. (2007). Revitalising the institution of awqaf in developing the community. In Singapore International Waqf Conference (pp. 1-27).

6.     Cizakca, M. (1995). Cash Waqfs of Bursa, 1555-1823. Journal of the Economic and Social History of the Orient, 38(3), 313-354.

7.     Cizakca, M. (2000). A history of philanthropic foundations: The Islamic world from the seventh century to the present. Istanbul: Bogazici University Press.

8.     Cizakca, M. (2011). Islamic Capitalism and Finance: Origins, Evolution and the Future. Edward Elgar Publishing.

9.     Kahf, M. (1998). Financing the development of awqaf property. In Seminar on Development of Awqaf (pp. 2-4).

10.     Kahf, M. (2007). The role of waqf in improving the ummah welfare. In Singapore International Waqf Conference 2007 (pp. 1-26).

## Chapter 13: Waqf and Education

The intersection of waqf (Islamic endowment) and education has been a cornerstone of Islamic civilization for centuries, playing a crucial role in the establishment and sustainability of educational institutions. This chapter explores the historical significance of waqf in education, the challenges faced by modern educational waqf projects, the role of government partnerships, and successful case studies that demonstrate the enduring impact of waqf on educational development.

## Historical Role of Waqf in Establishing Educational Institutions

The practice of using waqf to support education dates back to the early days of Islam. Waqf institutions served as financial resources for Islamic educational activities, enabling rapid evolution and expansion of educational facilities. This system reached its zenith during the golden age of Islam, when the needs of the educational world were adequately met through waqf endowments.

## Early Development of Educational Waqf

The concept of educational waqf gained prominence during the Abbasid Caliphate. Caliph al-Ma'mun is credited with first proposing the establishment of waqf agencies to support scientific activities. He argued that the continuity of scholarly pursuits should not solely depend on state subsidies or the philanthropy of rulers but should also involve public participation in bearing educational costs.

This initiative was later expanded by subsequent caliphs and princes, becoming a necessity in establishing scientific and cultural institutions funded by permanent endowments. The practice spread beyond Baghdad to other Islamic regions, with notable patrons such as Ibn Killis in Fatimid Egypt establishing academies and allocating substantial funds for their operation.

**Types of Educational Institutions Supported by Waqf:** Several types of educational institutions benefited from waqf support:

1. Maktab and Kuttab: These elementary schools were widespread across the Muslim world. In Palermo alone, 300 such schools were reported in the 10th century.

2. Jami' Mosques: These mosques served as centers for teaching both religious sciences and adab studies (literature and humanities) as early as the 8th century.

3. Madrasas: These colleges emerged as a development of the mosque-khan model, becoming recognizable institutions of higher learning.

4. Libraries: Waqf endowments also supported the establishment and maintenance of libraries, crucial for preserving and disseminating knowledge.

**Impact on Educational Access and Quality:** Waqf played a pivotal role in democratizing education in the Islamic world. It provided financial support for:

- Construction and maintenance of educational buildings
- Provision of learning materials and libraries
- Salaries for teachers
- Scholarships for students
- Accommodation for students from distant regions

This comprehensive support system ensured that education was accessible to a broad spectrum of society, regardless of economic status. The quality of education was also maintained through the consistent funding provided by waqf endowments.

**Notable Examples**

One striking example of waqf's impact on education is the case of Badr ibn Hasanawaih al-Kurdi, a wealthy nobleman who founded 3,000 mosques with academies, each equipped with a dormitory (mosque khan) financed through waqf. Similarly, Nidham al-Mulk allocated substantial waqf assets to his madrasas, ensuring their long-term sustainability.

The Al-Azhar University in Cairo stands as a testament to the enduring power of educational waqf. Established in 970 AD, it has been sustained for over a millennium through waqf endowments, providing free or subsidized education to students from across the Muslim world.

## Modern Challenges in Educational Waqf Projects:

While the historical impact of waqf on education is undeniable, modern educational waqf projects face several challenges that hinder their effectiveness and efficiency.

## Financial Constraints

One of the primary challenges is the limited sources of financing for waqf projects. The higher education waqf ecosystem requires diverse financing channels and instruments, which must be Shariah-compliant, to boost participation from both public and private sector donors. The growth of waqf assets is often hampered by fund liquidity issues.

**Administrative and Management Issues:** Many waqf institutions face administrative challenges, including:

- Lack of professional management expertise in waqf administration
- Inconsistent distribution of waqf benefits to beneficiaries
- Difficulties in determining the best type of development for waqf assets

These issues can lead to inefficiencies in the utilization of waqf resources and delays in project implementation.

## Legal and Regulatory Hurdles

In some jurisdictions, outdated or inadequate legal frameworks governing waqf can impede the development and management of educational waqf projects. Issues such as unsettled waqf land registration can lead to legal disputes, potentially disrupting the flow of benefits to educational institutions.

## Technological Gaps

There is often minimal technological input in waqf management. This lack of modern technology adoption can hinder efficient administration, transparency, and the ability to reach a wider donor base.

## Socio-cultural Challenges

Cultural beliefs sometimes hinder new marketing approaches for waqf promotion. The perception that religious matters should not be aggressively promoted can limit public awareness and participation in educational waqf projects.

## Environmental Considerations

Less attention is often given to environmental or green-waqf initiatives. As sustainability becomes increasingly important in education, this gap may need to be addressed in future waqf projects.

## Long-term Sustainability

Ensuring the long-term sustainability of educational waqf projects remains a challenge. Waqf project development often takes time to complete, causing delays in the distribution of benefits to beneficiaries. This can create difficulties in meeting the immediate economic, financial, and social needs of educational institutions and their students.

**Government Partnerships in Education through Waqf:** Recognizing the potential of waqf in addressing educational needs, many governments have begun to actively partner with and support educational waqf initiatives.

## Regulatory Frameworks

Governments play a crucial role in establishing and updating regulatory frameworks for waqf management. In Malaysia, for example, the government has implemented regulatory frameworks to ensure transparency and accountability in waqf education institutions. These frameworks help to standardize waqf management practices and build public trust in the system.

## Financial Assistance

Some governments provide financial assistance to support educational waqf projects. This can take the form of matching grants, tax incentives for donors, or direct funding for specific initiatives. Such support can significantly enhance the impact and reach of educational waqf projects.

## Capacity Building

Governments can contribute to the development of educational waqf by providing training and capacity-building programs for waqf administrators. This helps to professionalize waqf management and improve the efficiency of educational waqf projects.

## Collaboration with Private Sector

Government agencies often facilitate collaborations between educational waqf institutions and private sector entities. For instance, in Malaysia, corporate entities like Johor Corporation Berhad (JCorp) and its subsidiary, Waqaf An-Nur Corporation Berhad (WANCorp), have played significant roles in enhancing educational waqfs.

## Integration with National Education Policies

Some governments have integrated waqf into their national education policies. This integration ensures that waqf-based educational initiatives align with broader educational goals and standards, enhancing their relevance and impact.

## Research and Development

Government support for research on waqf and its applications in education can lead to innovations in waqf management and utilization. This research can inform policy decisions and help in developing best practices for educational waqf projects.

**Case Studies of Successful Educational Waqf Projects:** Several case studies demonstrate the successful implementation of educational waqf projects in various parts of the world.

## Al-Azhar University, Egypt

Al-Azhar University in Cairo is one of the oldest and most renowned examples of a successful educational waqf project. Established in 970 AD, it has been sustained for over a millennium through waqf endowments. The university's waqf funds cover expenses for faculty, student housing, libraries, and even food, allowing it to focus on academic excellence rather than relying on external funding[8]. Al-Azhar's success demonstrates how a well-managed waqf can sustain an institution's operations for centuries, establishing a legacy of learning and scholarship that benefits generations.

## Pondok Modern Darussalam Gontor, Indonesia

Pondok Modern Darussalam Gontor (PMDSG) in Indonesia is a prime example of a successful waqf-oriented educational institution. PMDSG's waqf-based education model provides immense benefits to the community at large. The institution's administration of waqf is implemented in a modern, professional, transparent, systematic, and well-planned manner. This model demonstrates how traditional Islamic concepts can be adapted to meet contemporary educational needs.

## International Islamic University Malaysia (IIUM)

The International Islamic University Malaysia (IIUM) has successfully implemented a waqf-based financing model to support its operations and development. The university established the IIUM Endowment Fund, which operates on waqf principles, to generate sustainable income for various educational initiatives. This model has helped IIUM reduce its dependence on government funding and enhance its financial sustainability.

## Turkish Educational Waqfs

Turkey has a long-standing tradition of educational waqfs. The country's Directorate of Religious Affairs oversees numerous waqf-funded educational institutions, including universities and vocational training centers. These institutions demonstrate how waqf can be integrated into a modern, secular educational system while maintaining its Islamic principles.

## Suleymaniye Complex, Turkey

While not exclusively an educational institution, the Suleymaniye Complex in Istanbul provides an excellent historical example of a comprehensive waqf project that included educational components. Built in the 16th century, the complex included a mosque, a hospital, a school, and a public kitchen, all funded by an extensive waqf. The school offered free education, demonstrating how waqf could address multiple societal needs, including education, within a single project.

## Malaysian University Waqf Initiatives

Several universities in Malaysia have successfully implemented waqf-based financing models. For instance, the University of Malaya established a waqf fund to support its operations and provide scholarships to students. Similarly, the International Islamic University Malaysia (IIUM) and Universiti Sains Islam Malaysia (USIM) have developed waqf funds to enhance their financial sustainability and support various educational initiatives.

These case studies highlight the diverse applications of waqf in education across different contexts and time periods. They demonstrate that when properly managed and supported, educational waqf projects can provide sustainable, high-quality education while remaining true to Islamic principles of charity and community development.

In conclusion, the role of waqf in education has been significant throughout Islamic history and continues to offer potential solutions to modern educational challenges. While facing various obstacles, educational waqf projects, when supported by effective government partnerships and managed professionally, can provide sustainable and accessible education. The successful case studies presented here serve as models for future initiatives, demonstrating the enduring relevance of waqf in addressing educational needs in Muslim societies and beyond.

**References:**


1.   http://repository.uinsa.ac.id/id/eprint/685/1/Hanun%20Asrohah_Waqf%20and%20its%20contribution%20in%20education.pdf

2.   http://ijhess.com/index.php/ijhess/article/download/791/631/7470

3.   https://www.researchgate.net/publication/334524405_The_Role_of_Waqf_in_Educational_Development_-_Evidence_from_Malaysia

4.   https://conference.uis.edu.my/icomm/9th/images/eproceeding/icomm9_005.pdf

5.   http://www.gbmrjournal.com/pdf/v16n2s/V16N2s-12.pdf

6.   https://muslimmirror.com/role-of-waqf-in-the-promotion-of-higher-education-in-india/

7.   https://iaeme.com/MasterAdmin/Journal_uploads/

IJCIET/VOLUME_10_ISSUE_2/IJCIET_10_02_078.pdf

8.      https://iaeme.com/MasterAdmin/Journal_uploads/ IJCIET/VOLUME_9_ISSUE_3/IJCIET_09_03_055.pdf

9.      https://www.iwaqf.io/post/case-studies-of-successful-waqf-projects-around-the-world

## Chapter 14: Waqf and Healthcare

Waqf, an Islamic endowment system, has played a significant role in supporting healthcare services throughout Islamic history and continues to do so in many Muslim-majority countries today. This chapter explores the multifaceted relationship between waqf and healthcare, examining its historical contributions, current applications, challenges, and potential for future development.

### Role of Waqf in Funding Hospitals and Clinics

Waqf has been instrumental in funding healthcare facilities and services since the early days of Islam. Hospitals, clinics, medical schools, and pharmacies have historically been supported by waqf endowments. This tradition continues in modern times, with waqf playing a crucial role in establishing and maintaining healthcare institutions.

### Funding Healthcare Facilities

The establishment and maintenance of hospitals, clinics, and other healthcare institutions can be funded through waqf. This practice ensures a sustainable source of funding for these essential services. Historically, numerous hospitals have been built and operated through waqf endowments, providing vital medical services to communities.

In Malaysia, for example, the State Islamic Religious Council has been using waqf funds to support healthcare services. Initiatives include the establishment of dialysis centers, procurement of medical equipment, provision of medications, and creation of waqf clinics. These efforts demonstrate the potential for waqf to enhance a country's healthcare system and reduce the financial burden on both the government and citizens.

### Financing Healthcare Education

Waqf can also be used to finance medical education,

scholarships, and training programs for healthcare professionals. This ensures that communities have access to qualify and skilled medical personnel to meet their healthcare needs. By investing in healthcare education, waqf contributes to the long-term sustainability and quality of healthcare services.

## Providing Healthcare for the Needy

One of the most important roles of waqf in healthcare is providing services to those who cannot afford them. Waqf can be utilized to offer free or subsidized medical services to the underprivileged, ensuring that access to quality healthcare is not limited by financial constraints. This aligns with the Islamic principle of social responsibility and caring for the less fortunate members of society.

## Challenges in Managing Healthcare Waqf Properties

Despite its potential, the management of healthcare waqf properties faces several challenges that need to be addressed to maximize its impact.

## Mismanagement and Financial Irregularities

One of the primary challenges is the mismanagement of waqf properties and funds. Issues such as financial irregularities within waqf boards, improper registration, and misuse of income have adversely affected the Muslim community and the potential beneficiaries of healthcare waqf. These problems undermine the effectiveness of waqf in supporting healthcare services and erode public trust in waqf institutions.

## Illegal Encroachments

Many waqf properties, including those designated for healthcare purposes, have been illegally occupied. While legal measures have been taken to address this issue, they are often insufficient to fully resolve the problem. The illegal occupation of waqf properties reduces the resources available for healthcare services and complicates the management of these assets.

## Misuse of Income

The income generated from waqf properties is sometimes not entirely spent on the intended charitable purposes, including healthcare. This leads to a lack of education, health, and welfare services in some areas. Proper allocation and utilization of waqf income are crucial for ensuring that healthcare services receive the necessary funding.

## Lack of Transparency and Accountability

The management of waqf properties, including those designated for healthcare often lacks transparency and accountability. This can lead to corruption and misuse of resources. Implementing robust governance structures and transparent reporting mechanisms is essential for ensuring that waqf assets are used effectively for healthcare purposes.

## Collaboration with Government Healthcare Programs

Collaboration between waqf institutions and government healthcare programs presents an opportunity to enhance the impact of waqf in the healthcare sector. Such partnerships can leverage the strengths of both systems to provide better healthcare services to the public.

## Public-Private Partnerships

Waqf institutions can collaborate with government public healthcare agencies, such as hospitals, to offer numerous benefits to multi-religious, multi-racial citizens. This collaboration can take the form of public-private partnerships (PPPs), where waqf funds and assets complement government resources to improve healthcare delivery.

## Reducing Government Expenditure

By supporting healthcare services, waqf can help reduce

government expenditure on healthcare. This is particularly important in developing countries where healthcare budgets are often strained. Waqf can provide an alternative source of funding for healthcare infrastructure, equipment, and services, allowing governments to allocate their resources more efficiently.

## Enhancing Healthcare Quality and Accessibility

Collaboration between waqf institutions and public healthcare providers can lead to improved healthcare quality at affordable costs. For example, waqf funds can be used to upgrade hospital equipment or improve facilities, resulting in better patient care. Additionally, waqf-supported healthcare services can often provide care at lower costs or even free of charge to those in need, increasing accessibility to quality healthcare.

## Challenges in Collaboration

While collaboration between waqf institutions and government healthcare programs holds great potential, it also faces challenges. These may include differences in management styles, regulatory issues, and concerns about maintaining the religious character of waqf-funded healthcare services. Developing clear frameworks for collaboration and addressing these challenges is crucial for successful partnerships.

**Historical Contributions of Waqf to Health Services:** The historical contributions of waqf to health services are significant and provide valuable insights into its potential for contemporary healthcare systems.

## Early Islamic Hospitals

Waqf played a crucial role in funding healthcare facilities and services since the early days of Islam. The first large hospital in Islamic civilization was the Bimaristan established by Harun al-Rashid in Baghdad in the late 8th century CE. These early hospitals, funded by waqf, offered free medical care regardless of social status, religion, or nationality.

## Golden Age of Islamic Medicine

During the Islamic Golden Age, waqf-funded hospitals (known as Bimaristans or Maristans) were at the forefront of medical care and education. These institutions were staffed by skilled physicians and surgeons, supported by waqf revenues. They not only provided medical care but also played a vital role in medical education, fostering the training of future generations of healthcare professionals.

## Specialized Healthcare Facilities

Muslims established specialized hospitals for certain diseases, including leprosy hospitals for isolating and treating patients away from society, and psychiatric hospitals dedicated to clinically and psychologically treating mental health patients. These specialized facilities demonstrate the comprehensive approach to healthcare supported by waqf.

## Widespread Impact

The impact of waqf on healthcare was widespread across the Islamic world. In Cordoba, Spain, for example, there were fifty hospitals endowed and funded by caliphs, princes, and wealthy individuals. Similarly, in Morocco, large hospitals were established in major cities, extensively discussed by historians.

## Innovation in Healthcare Delivery

Interestingly, some waqf-funded hospitals incorporated innovative approaches to patient care. For instance, part of the waqf for Sidi Faraj Hospital in Fez, Morocco, was designated for treating storks, and a portion for musicians who visited the hospital once a week to entertain patients. This holistic approach to healthcare, considering both physical and mental well-being, was ahead of its time.

In conclusion, waqf has played a crucial role in funding

and supporting healthcare services throughout Islamic history and continues to hold significant potential for addressing contemporary healthcare challenges. By addressing the challenges in managing healthcare waqf properties and fostering collaboration with government healthcare programs, waqf can continue to make substantial contributions to improving healthcare access and quality, particularly for underserved populations. The historical contributions of waqf to health services provide valuable lessons and inspiration for leveraging this Islamic institution to meet modern healthcare needs.

**References:**


1. Ascarya, A., & Tanjung, H. (2021). Issues and challenges of waqf in providing healthcare resources. International Journal of Ethics and Systems, 38(4), 598-615.

2. Baqutayan, S. M. S., & Mahdzir, A. M. (2018). Waqf and healthcare: Past, present and future. International Journal of Academic Research in Business and Social Sciences, 8(12), 1-14.

3. Fahruroji, F. (2020). The role of waqf in healthcare: A case study of Waqf An-Nur Corporation Berhad in Malaysia. Journal of Islamic Economics, 12(2), 217-232.

4. Halal Times. (2023). What Is the Role of Waqf in Healthcare? Retrieved from https://www.halaltimes.com/what-is-the-role-of-waqf-in-healthcare/

5. IBW Waqf. (2024). The Role of Islamic Waqf in the Health Sector. Retrieved from https://ibwaqf.org.uk/news/blog/the-role-of-islamic-waqf-in-the-health-sector

6. Milli Gazette. (2024). Challenges around Waqf in India. Retrieved from https://www.milligazette.com/news/6-issues/34121-challenges-around-waqf-in-india/

7. Press Information Bureau. (2023). Explainer on Waqf Amendment Bill 2024. Retrieved from https://pib.gov.in/

PressNoteDetails.aspx?NoteId=152139&ModuleId=3

117

# Chapter 15: Waqf and Religious Institutions

Waqf, an Islamic endowment system, has played a crucial role in the development and maintenance of religious institutions throughout Islamic history. This chapter explores the multifaceted aspects of waqf in relation to religious institutions, focusing on the maintenance of mosques and dargahs, challenges in religious property management, legal issues surrounding religious waqf properties, and the role of waqf in preserving Islamic heritage.

## Maintenance of Mosques and Dargahs through Waqf

The concept of waqf has been instrumental in the establishment and maintenance of mosques and dargahs (shrines) since the early days of Islam. The practice of dedicating property for religious purposes can be traced back to the time of Prophet Muhammad, who encouraged his followers to establish endowments for the benefit of the community.

## Mosques as Waqf Properties

Mosques have been one of the primary beneficiaries of the waqf system. The first known waqf in Islamic history was the Quba Mosque in Medina, built upon the Prophet's arrival in the city. This set a precedent for the establishment of mosques through waqf endowments, a practice that continued throughout Islamic history.

The waqf system ensured the continuous maintenance and operation of mosques by providing a sustainable source of funding. Waqf properties dedicated to mosques typically included:

1. The mosque building itself

2. Adjacent lands for expansion or auxiliary services

3. Income-generating properties to support operational costs

For instance, during the Ottoman period, the Süleymaniye complex in Istanbul was supported by extensive waqf properties, which funded not only the mosque but also associated institutions such as schools and hospitals.

## Dargahs and Waqf

Dargahs, the shrines of Sufi saints, have also benefited significantly from the waqf system. These spiritual centers often received endowments from devotees, which helped in their maintenance and expansion. The waqf properties associated with dargahs typically included:

1. The shrine building

2. Surrounding land for pilgrims' accommodation

3. Agricultural lands or other income-generating assets

The income from these waqf properties was used to maintain the shrine, provide for the caretakers, and often support charitable activities associated with the dargah.

**Challenges in Maintenance:** While the waqf system has been crucial in maintaining mosques and dargahs, it has faced several challenges:

1. Mismanagement: Issues of financial irregularities and corruption within waqf boards have affected the proper maintenance of religious properties.

2. Encroachment: Many waqf properties, including those associated with mosques and dargahs, have been illegally occupied, reducing the income available for maintenance.

3. Lack of Documentation: Many historical mosques and dargahs have been used by Muslims for generations without formal documentation. The concept of "waqf by user" recognized these properties, but recent legal changes have put their status in

question.

4. Insufficient Funds: Despite the extensive waqf properties, many mosques and dargahs struggle with insufficient funds for maintenance due to low rental yields or misuse of income.

## Challenges in Religious Property Management

The management of religious properties through the waqf system faces numerous challenges in contemporary times. These challenges stem from historical, legal, and administrative issues that have accumulated over time.

## Administrative Challenges

1. Centralized Control: The establishment of state Waqf Boards in India, for instance, has led to a centralized control system that often lacks the flexibility to address local needs effectively.

2. Lack of Expertise: Many Waqf Boards lack the necessary expertise in property management, leading to suboptimal utilization of waqf assets.

3. Transparency Issues: There have been persistent concerns about the lack of transparency in the management of waqf properties, leading to mistrust and reduced public participation.

## Financial Challenges

1. Low Yield: Many waqf properties, especially those leased out long ago, generate minimal income due to outdated rental agreements.

2. Misuse of Income: The income generated from waqf properties is often not entirely spent on the intended charitable purposes, leading to a lack of funds for maintenance and development.

3. Limited Investment: The traditional interpretation of waqf laws has sometimes limited the ability to invest in or develop waqf properties to increase their yield.

## Legal and Regulatory Challenges

1. Complex Legal Framework: The legal framework governing waqf properties is often complex and varies across different regions, making uniform management difficult.

2. Disputes over Property Rights: There are frequent disputes over the ownership and control of waqf properties, leading to lengthy legal battles.

3. Changing Regulations: Frequent changes in waqf laws and regulations create uncertainty and challenges in long-term planning for property management.

## Social and Cultural Challenges

1. Resistance to Change: There is often resistance from traditional stakeholders to modernize the management of waqf properties.

2. Lack of Community Involvement: In many cases, there is a lack of active community involvement in the management and development of waqf properties.

3. Sectarian Issues: In some cases, sectarian differences within the Muslim community have led to disputes over the control and management of waqf properties.

**Legal Issues Surrounding Religious Waqf Properties:** The legal landscape surrounding religious waqf properties is complex and often contentious, reflecting the intersection of religious law, state legislation, and historical practices.

**Legal Framework:** In India, the primary legislation governing waqf properties is the Waqf Act of 1995, which replaced the earlier Waqf Act of 1954. This act provides a comprehensive legal framework for the management and supervision of waqf properties. Key aspects of this legal framework include:

1. Mandatory Registration: The Act mandates the registration of

all waqf properties with the state Waqf Boards.

2. Waqf Tribunals: Special tribunals have been established to adjudicate disputes related to waqf properties.

3. Survey of Waqf Properties: The Act provides for a comprehensive survey of waqf properties to identify and protect them.

**Current Legal Challenges**

1. Proposed Amendments: Recent proposals to amend the Waqf Act have sparked controversy. These amendments include:

- Stripping Waqf Boards of their powers to declare properties as waqf
- Introducing non-Muslim members into Waqf Boards
- Granting district collectors authority over waqf properties

2. Waqf by User: The concept of "waqf by user," which recognized properties used for religious purposes over long periods as waqf, is under threat in proposed amendments. This could affect the status of many historical mosques and dargahs.

3. Property Disputes: There are numerous ongoing legal disputes over the ownership and control of waqf properties. These often involve conflicts between Waqf Boards, government agencies, and private parties.

4. Encroachment Issues: Legal battles to reclaim encroached waqf properties are common and often protracted.

**Constitutional and Human Rights Issues**

1. Religious Autonomy: There are ongoing debates about the extent to which the state can intervene in the management of religious endowments without infringing on religious freedoms guaranteed by the constitution.

2. Minority Rights: As waqf is primarily associated with the

Muslim community in countries like India, legal issues often intersect with questions of minority rights and protections.

3. Gender Equality: Traditional interpretations of waqf law have sometimes been challenged on grounds of gender equality, particularly regarding the management and beneficiaries of waqf properties.

## International Legal Perspectives

While the legal issues discussed above are primarily in the Indian context, similar challenges are faced in other countries with significant Muslim populations. There is a growing interest in developing international standards for waqf management that balance religious principles with modern legal and governance norms.

## Role of Waqf in Preserving Islamic Heritage

Waqf has played a crucial role in preserving Islamic heritage throughout history. This role extends beyond mere financial support to encompass the physical preservation of historical sites, the continuation of religious and cultural practices, and the transmission of Islamic knowledge.

## Preservation of Historical Sites

1. Architectural Heritage: Waqf endowments have been instrumental in preserving numerous historical mosques, madrasas, and other Islamic buildings. For example, the Al-Azhar Mosque and University in Cairo, one of the oldest continuously operating educational institutions in the world, have been maintained through waqf for over a thousand years.

2. Restoration and Maintenance: Income from waqf properties has funded the restoration and maintenance of historical Islamic sites. This has been crucial in preserving architectural styles and techniques that might otherwise have been lost.

3. Protection from Development: By designating properties

as waqf, many historical sites have been protected from commercial development or repurposing, ensuring their preservation for future generations.

## Continuation of Religious and Cultural Practices

1. Support for Religious Rituals: Waqf endowments have ensured the continuation of religious practices by providing for the needs of mosques, including the salaries of imams and muezzins, and the costs of religious ceremonies.

2. Preservation of Manuscripts: Many waqf-supported institutions have played a crucial role in preserving Islamic manuscripts and rare books. For instance, the Süleymaniye Library in Istanbul houses thousands of valuable manuscripts preserved through waqf endowments.

3. Cultural Festivals: Waqf properties often support the continuation of cultural festivals and religious celebrations, helping to maintain local traditions and practices.

## Transmission of Islamic Knowledge

1. Educational Institutions: Waqf has been a primary source of funding for Islamic educational institutions, from primary schools (maktabs) to advanced centers of learning (madrasas). This has ensured the continuous transmission of Islamic knowledge across generations.

2. Scholarships: Many waqf endowments have been specifically dedicated to providing scholarships for students of Islamic sciences, enabling the education of scholars who would further preserve and develop Islamic heritage.

3. Libraries and Research Centers: Waqf-supported libraries and research centers have played a crucial role in preserving Islamic texts and facilitating ongoing research into Islamic history and culture.

**Challenges in Heritage Preservation:** Despite its historical significance, the role of waqf in preserving Islamic heritage faces several contemporary challenges:

1. Financial Constraints: Many historical waqf properties struggle with insufficient funds for proper preservation and maintenance.

2. Modernization Pressures: There is often tension between preserving historical sites and the pressure to modernize or repurpose properties for contemporary needs.

3. Lack of Expertise: Proper preservation of historical sites requires specialized knowledge, which is not always available within traditional waqf management structures.

4. Legal and Administrative Issues: Complex legal frameworks and administrative challenges can hinder effective heritage preservation efforts.

**Future Prospects:** Despite these challenges, there are promising developments in the use of waqf for heritage preservation:

1. Digital Preservation: Some waqf institutions are embracing digital technologies to preserve and make accessible historical manuscripts and documents.

2. International Cooperation: There are growing efforts to foster international cooperation in the preservation of Islamic heritage sites, including those supported by waqf.

3. Innovative Financing: New models of waqf financing, including cash waqfs and waqf-linked sukuk (Islamic bonds), offer potential for increased funding for heritage preservation.

In conclusion, waqf continues to play a vital role in the maintenance of religious institutions and the preservation of Islamic heritage. However, it faces significant challenges in terms of property management and legal issues. Addressing these challenges through modernization of management practices, legal reforms, and innovative financing models will be crucial for ensuring that waqf can continue to fulfill its historical role in supporting religious institutions and preserving Islamic heritage in the contemporary world.

## References:


1. BBC News. (2024, November 28). Why Muslims in India are opposing changes to a property law. https://www.bbc.com/news/articles/c704d73kjpwo

2. Mahawakf. (n.d.). FAQ. https://mahawakf.com/faq/

3. The Milli Gazette. (2024, September 17). Challenges around Waqf in India. https://www.milligazette.com/news/6-issues/34121-challenges-around-waqf-in-india/

4. Omar, M. (n.d.). Waqf - an economic perspective. Bank for International Settlements. https://www.bis.org/review/r180411b.htm

5. Wikipedia. (2024, November 5). Waqf. https://en.wikipedia.org/wiki/Waqf

6. The India Forum. (2024, November 25). Wakf Reforms, or a Bid to Control Waqf Properties? https://www.theindiaforum.in/law/wakf-reforms-or-bid-control-waqf-properties

7. India Foundation. (n.d.). Unveiling Bias: Governance Structures in India's Religious Institutions. https://indiafoundation.in/articles-and-commentaries/unveiling-bias-governance-structures-in-indias-religious-institutions/

8. Hayatullah. (2021, December 20). Revisiting the Concept of Waqf: Its Maintenance, Issues and ... http://journalarticle.ukm.my/18225/1/Hayatullah-IJIT-20-Dec-2021.pdf

9. Babacan, M. (2011). Economics of philanthropic institutions, regulation and governance in Turkey. Journal of Economic and Social Research, 13(2), 61-89.

10. Press Information Bureau. (2023, July 24). Explainer on Waqf Amendment Bill 2024. https://pib.gov.in/

PressNoteDetails.aspx?NoteId=152139&ModuleId=3
11.             Al    Baraka    Forum. (2024, August 13). ROLE OF WAQF IN SOCIO-ECONOMIC DEVELOPMENT. https://forum.albaraka.site/role-of-waqf-in-socio-economic-development/?lang=en
12.          FasterCapital. (n.d.). The Significance Of Waqf In Islamic Culture And Society. https://fastercapital.com/topics/the-significance-of-waqf-in-islamic-culture-and-society.html

---

## *Chapter 16: Modernization of Waqf Management*

The modernization of waqf management represents a significant shift in the administration and utilization of Islamic endowments. This chapter explores the various aspects of this modernization process, focusing on the use of technology, digitization of records, the role of artificial intelligence, and global best practices in waqf administration.

### Use of Technology in Waqf Administration

The integration of technology in waqf administration has revolutionized the way these endowments are managed, leading to increased efficiency, transparency, and accountability. The adoption of digital tools and platforms has enabled waqf institutions to streamline their operations, improve decision-making processes, and enhance their overall impact.

One of the primary benefits of technology in waqf administration is the improvement in operational efficiency. By automating various administrative processes, such as record-keeping, asset management, and financial reporting, waqf institutions can significantly reduce operational costs and minimize human error (Kasmon et al., 2024). This automation not only saves time and resources but also allows waqf administrators to focus on more strategic aspects of their work, such as developing innovative waqf instruments and expanding their reach.

The use of technology has also facilitated better asset management. Digital platforms provide waqf managers with accurate data and analytical tools, enabling them to make more informed decisions regarding the allocation and utilization of waqf assets (Agaileh, 2024). This data-driven approach to asset management can lead to more effective and efficient use of waqf resources, ultimately maximizing the social impact of these endowments.

Furthermore, technology has played a crucial role in enhancing transparency and accountability in waqf administration. Digital platforms allow for real-time monitoring and reporting of waqf activities, making it easier for stakeholders to track the utilization of funds and the performance of waqf assets (Kasmon et al., 2024). This increased transparency not only builds trust among donors and beneficiaries but also helps prevent mismanagement and fraud.

The adoption of blockchain technology in waqf administration represents another significant advancement. Blockchain can be used to create smart contracts linked to waqf projects, facilitating fundraising and ensuring secure and transparent transfer of ownership for waqf contributions (Rabbani & Khan, 2020, as cited in Kasmon et al., 2024). This technology has the potential to revolutionize the way waqf assets are managed and distributed, particularly in the context of cross-border waqf initiatives.

## Digitization of Records and Property Listings

The digitization of waqf records and property listings is a crucial aspect of modernizing waqf management. This process involves converting physical documents and records into digital formats, creating comprehensive databases of waqf properties, and implementing Geographic Information System (GIS) mapping for better asset tracking and management.

In India, the Ministry of Minority Affairs has made significant progress in this area through the implementation of the Waqf Assets Management System of India (WAMSI). This dedicated online portal has been developed for the computerization and digitization of waqf property records, as well as for GIS mapping of waqf properties to prevent encroachment (Press Information Bureau, 2021). As of December 2021, records of 775,172 immovable waqf properties had been registered in the WAMSI

Registration Module, with GIS mapping completed for 219,230 properties.

The digitization process offers numerous benefits for waqf administration. Firstly, it ensures the preservation of historical waqf records, protecting them from physical deterioration and potential loss. Secondly, it facilitates easier access to and retrieval of information, enabling waqf administrators to make more informed decisions regarding asset management and utilization. Thirdly, digital records and property listings enhance transparency and accountability, as they can be easily audited and monitored by relevant authorities and stakeholders.

Moreover, the digitization of waqf records contributes to better asset protection. By creating comprehensive digital inventories of waqf properties, including their locations and legal status, waqf institutions can more effectively prevent encroachment and unauthorized use of waqf assets. This is particularly important given the historical challenges faced by many waqf institutions in protecting their properties from misappropriation or neglect.

The process of digitization also facilitates better coordination and information sharing among various waqf institutions and regulatory bodies. For instance, in the United Arab Emirates, the Federal Waqf Law No. 5 of 2018 provides a legal framework for the management of waqf properties, and the digitization of records supports the implementation of this law by enabling more effective oversight and coordination (Agaileh, 2024).

**Role of Artificial Intelligence in Waqf Management**

Artificial Intelligence (AI) is emerging as a powerful tool in modernizing waqf management, offering innovative solutions to longstanding challenges in the sector. The integration of AI technologies in waqf administration has the potential to enhance decision-making processes, improve asset management, and increase the overall efficiency and effectiveness of waqf institutions.

One of the key applications of AI in waqf management is in data analysis and predictive modeling. By leveraging machine learning algorithms, waqf institutions can analyze vast amounts of data related to their assets, beneficiaries, and market conditions to identify patterns and trends. This can help in making more informed decisions regarding asset allocation, investment strategies, and program development (Kasmon et al., 2024).

AI can also play a significant role in risk management for waqf assets. By analyzing historical data and market trends, AI systems can help identify potential risks to waqf investments and suggest mitigation strategies. This is particularly important for waqf institutions that manage large and diverse portfolios of assets, as it can help ensure the long-term sustainability and growth of the waqf endowment.

Another promising application of AI in waqf management is in the area of beneficiary identification and impact assessment. AI algorithms can analyze demographic data, socioeconomic indicators, and other relevant factors to identify communities or individuals most in need of waqf support. This can help waqf institutions target their resources more effectively and maximize their social impact. Additionally, AI can be used to develop more sophisticated impact assessment tools, enabling waqf institutions to better measure and communicate the outcomes of their programs.

The use of AI in waqf management also extends to the realm of donor engagement and fundraising. AI-powered chatbots and virtual assistants can provide personalized information to potential donors, answer queries, and facilitate the donation process. Machine learning algorithms can also analyze donor behavior and preferences to develop more targeted and effective fundraising strategies (Kasmon et al., 2024)[3].

However, the integration of AI in waqf management also raises important ethical and governance considerations. It is crucial to ensure that AI systems are developed and deployed in a manner that aligns with Islamic principles and the fundamental objectives of waqf. This includes addressing issues of data privacy, algorithmic bias, and the potential displacement of human decision-making in waqf administration.

## Global Best Practices in Waqf Administration

As the waqf sector undergoes modernization, several global best practices have emerged in waqf administration. These practices draw from successful models implemented in various countries and reflect a growing emphasis on professionalism, transparency, and innovation in waqf management.

One of the key best practices is the adoption of professional management approaches. Countries like Kuwait and Singapore have set notable examples in this regard, applying modern management techniques competently and transparently (World Bank Group, 2019). These approaches include the implementation of robust governance structures, the development of clear strategic plans, and the adoption of performance measurement systems.

Another important best practice is the development of comprehensive regulatory frameworks for waqf administration. The United Arab Emirates, for instance, has implemented the Federal Waqf Law No. 5 of 2018, which provides a clear legal structure for waqf management and oversight (Agaileh, 2024). Such regulatory frameworks help ensure accountability, protect waqf assets, and facilitate the growth and development of the waqf sector.

The integration of waqf with modern financial instruments represents another global best practice. For example, the International Shari'ah Research Academy for Islamic Finance (ISRA) is working with the Islamic Development Bank to issue awqaf sukuk worth USD 100 million, which will be used to fund various social and economic development projects (World Bank Group, 2019). This innovative approach demonstrates how traditional waqf concepts can be combined with contemporary financial tools to mobilize resources and expand the impact of waqf.

Collaboration and knowledge sharing among waqf institutions is also emerging as a best practice. International conferences, research initiatives, and platforms for sharing experiences and best practices are helping to drive innovation and improvement in waqf administration globally. For instance, the World Bank Group, INCEIF, and ISRA have organized roundtable discussions on waqf, bringing together experts and practitioners to discuss successful waqf models that can be replicated globally (World Bank Group, 2019).

The development of standardized reporting and performance assessment measures is another important best practice in modern waqf administration. As waqf becomes more ubiquitous in Muslim societies, there is a growing need for standardized methods to evaluate the impact and effectiveness of waqf programs. This includes the development of key performance indicators (KPIs) specific to waqf institutions and the adoption of impact assessment frameworks that align with both Islamic principles and international development goals.

Lastly, the promotion of public awareness and education about waqf is increasingly recognized as a crucial aspect of effective waqf administration. Many waqf institutions are leveraging digital platforms and social media to educate the public about the concept of waqf, its potential impact, and opportunities for participation. This approach not only helps in mobilizing resources but also ensures the long-term sustainability of the waqf sector by fostering a culture of endowment and philanthropy.

In conclusion, the modernization of waqf management represents a significant opportunity to revitalize this important Islamic institution and enhance its impact in addressing contemporary social and economic challenges. By leveraging technology, embracing digitization, harnessing the power of artificial intelligence, and adopting global best practices, waqf institutions can significantly improve their efficiency, transparency, and effectiveness. However, this modernization process must be guided by a careful balance between innovation and adherence to the fundamental principles and objectives of waqf as established in Islamic law and tradition. As the waqf sector continues to evolve, ongoing research, collaboration, and adaptation will be crucial to ensuring that waqf remains a relevant and powerful tool for social and economic development in Muslim societies and beyond.

## References


1. Agaileh, Z. M. (2024). Educational waqf (endowment) in artificial intelligence programs: Toward a new form of waqf. Journal of Governance & Regulation, 13(1), 231–240. https://doi.org/10.22495/jgrv13i1art21

2. Kasmon, B., Ibrahim, S.S., Daud, D., Raja Hisham, R.R.I. and Ratnasari, R.T. (2024). Future behavior in waqf digitalization: integrating UTAUT and DIT. Journal of Islamic Marketing, Vol. ahead-of-print No. ahead-of-print. https://doi.org/10.1108/JIMA-03-2024-0111

3. Press Information Bureau. (2021, December 6). Computerization and Digitization of Wakf Records. Government of India. https://pib.gov.in/PressReleaseIframePage.aspx?PRID=1778484

4. World Bank Group. (2019). Maximizing Social Impact through Waqf Solutions. https://documents1.worldbank.org/curated/fr/930461562218730622/text/Maximizing-Social-Impact-Through-Waqf-Solutions.txt

# Chapter 17: State Intervention in Waqf Administration

State intervention in Waqf administration has been a contentious issue in India, sparking debates about the balance between religious autonomy and government oversight. This chapter explores the justifications for state involvement, criticisms of such intervention, the delicate balance between autonomy and regulation, and a comparative analysis with other countries.

## Justification for State Oversight

The Indian government's involvement in Waqf administration is primarily justified by the need to ensure proper management, transparency, and accountability in the handling of Waqf properties. The Waqf Act of 1995, along with subsequent amendments, provides the legal framework for this oversight.

One of the main arguments for state intervention is the vast scale and value of Waqf properties in India. With Waqf boards overseeing significant assets, there is a pressing need for effective management and protection against misuse or encroachment. The government's role is seen as crucial in safeguarding these properties for their intended religious and charitable purposes.

Another justification is the historical mismanagement and lack of transparency in some Waqf boards. Issues such as corruption, financial irregularities, and inefficient administration have plagued many Waqf institutions, necessitating external oversight. The government argues that its involvement can help address these systemic problems and improve the overall functioning of Waqf boards.

The need for modernization and professional management of Waqf properties is also cited as a reason for state intervention. Many Waqf boards lack the resources, expertise, or infrastructure to manage their assets effectively in the modern context. Government oversight is seen as a means to introduce better management practices, digitization of records, and more efficient administrative systems.

## Criticism of State Involvement in Waqf Matters

Despite the justifications, state involvement in Waqf administration has faced significant criticism from various quarters, including religious leaders, community representatives, and legal experts.

One of the primary criticisms is that state intervention infringes upon the religious autonomy guaranteed by the Indian Constitution. Critics argue that the management of Waqf properties, being inherently religious in nature, should remain under the control of the Muslim community. They contend that government involvement violates the principles of secularism and the right to religious freedom enshrined in Articles 25 and 26 of the Constitution.

The proposed amendments to the Waqf Act, particularly the Waqf (Amendment) Bill, 2024, have intensified these criticisms. The bill's provisions, such as including non-Muslim members in Waqf boards and centralizing power in government hands, are seen as direct assaults on the autonomy of Waqf institutions. Critics argue that these changes could lead to increased encroachments on Waqf properties and undermine the community's ability to assert its rights over these assets.

Another significant criticism is the perceived bias in the government's approach to different religious endowments. While Hindu temples in many states are under government control, critics argue that the level of intervention in Waqf affairs is disproportionate and discriminatory. This disparity is seen as a violation of the principle of equality before the law.

The effectiveness of state intervention is also questioned. Despite years of government oversight, many Waqf boards continue to face issues of mismanagement, corruption, and property encroachment. Critics argue that instead of solving problems, excessive government control has often led to bureaucratic inefficiencies and political interference.

**Balance between Autonomy and Regulation**

Finding the right balance between religious autonomy and necessary regulation is crucial in the context of Waqf administration. This balance must respect the religious nature of Waqf while ensuring proper management and accountability.

One approach to achieving this balance is through a system of co-governance, where the state provides oversight without direct control. This could involve setting up independent regulatory bodies that include both community representatives and government appointees. Such a system could help maintain the religious character of Waqf institutions while introducing professional management practices.

Transparency and accountability measures can be implemented without compromising religious autonomy. For instance, regular audits, public disclosure of financial statements, and the use of technology for property management can enhance transparency without direct state control.

Empowering Waqf boards with more resources and authority to manage their affairs effectively could reduce the need for extensive state intervention. This could include providing training and capacity building for Waqf board members and staff, as well as granting them more legal powers to protect and develop Waqf properties.

The role of the judiciary in maintaining this balance is also crucial. Courts can act as arbiters in disputes between Waqf boards and the government, ensuring that state intervention does not overstep constitutional boundaries.

## Comparative Analysis with Other Countries

A comparative analysis of Waqf administration in other countries provides valuable insights into alternative models of governance and regulation.

In Singapore, the Islamic Religious Council of Singapore (MUIS) serves as the central authority responsible for all Islamic affairs, including Waqf management. Singapore's model is characterized by a centralized, professional approach to Waqf administration. The country has implemented robust management practices, including the use of digital systems for property registration, lease management, and financial reporting. This approach has led to greater efficiency and transparency in Waqf administration.

Malaysia offers another model of Waqf governance, where state Islamic religious councils (SIRCs) manage Waqf properties. The Malaysian model combines elements of state oversight with religious autonomy, as SIRCs are semi-governmental bodies with a degree of independence.

In contrast to India's centralized approach, some countries have adopted more decentralized models. For example, in some Middle Eastern countries, Waqf administration is largely left to individual trustees or family custodians, with minimal state intervention.

The Turkish model presents an interesting case study. Turkey has a long history of state involvement in Waqf affairs, dating back to the Ottoman era. The country has recently undertaken reforms to modernize its Waqf system, balancing state oversight with increased autonomy for Waqf institutions.

These international examples demonstrate that there is no one-size-fits-all approach to Waqf administration. Each country's model is shaped by its historical, cultural, and legal context.

However, common themes emerge across successful models, including transparency, professional management, and a balance between state oversight and religious autonomy.

In conclusion, state intervention in Waqf administration in India remains a complex and contentious issue. While there are valid justifications for government oversight, concerns about religious autonomy and the effectiveness of state intervention persist. The challenge lies in finding a balanced approach that ensures proper management and accountability of Waqf properties while respecting their religious nature and the rights of the Muslim community. Learning from international examples and adapting best practices to the Indian context could help in developing a more effective and acceptable model of Waqf governance.

**References:**


1. PRS India. (n.d.). The Waqf (Amendment) Bill, 2024. Retrieved from https://prsindia.org/billtrack/the-waqf-amendment-bill-2024

2. India Foundation. (n.d.). Unveiling Bias: Governance Structures in India's Religious Institutions. Retrieved from https://indiafoundation.in/articles-and-commentaries/unveiling-bias-governance-structures-in-indias-religious-institutions/

3. The Economic Times. (2024, August 8). Waqf Act: 'Waqt' for Waqf to change? How the battlelines are drawn. Retrieved from https://economictimes.indiatimes.com/news/india/waqf-act-waqt-for-waqf-to-change-how-the-battlelines-are-drawn/articleshow/112371898.cms

4. Owais, M., & Manaf, Z. I. A. (2023). Comparative Analysis of Waqf Institutions Governance in India and Singapore. El Barka: Journal of Islamic Economics and Business, 6(2), 257-282.

5. Central Waqf Council. (2017). Information Handbook under RTI ACT. Retrieved from https://

centralwaqfcouncil.gov.in/sites/default/files/ Information%20Handbook%20under%20RTI%20ACT-Updated-09-10-2017_0.pdf

6.          The India Forum. (2024, November 25). Wakf Reforms, or a Bid to Control Waqf Properties? Retrieved from https://www.theindiaforum.in/law/wakf-reforms-or-bid-control-waqf-properties

7.          Telangana Today. (2024, September 30). Opinion: Challenges with Waqf Bill. Retrieved from https:// telanganatoday.com/opinion-challenges-with-waqf-bill

8.          Radiance Weekly. (2024, August 27). The Waqf (Amendment) Bill 2024 Raises Concerns Among Muslims. Retrieved from https://radianceweekly.net/waqf-slips-into-government-hands-the-waqf-amendment-bill-2024-raises-concerns-among-muslims/

---

## *Chapter 18: Waqf and the Indian Constitution*

The intersection of waqf (Islamic religious endowments) and the Indian Constitution presents a complex legal and social landscape that touches on fundamental rights, religious freedoms, and the secular nature of the Indian state. This chapter explores the various dimensions of this relationship, examining how waqf institutions fit within India's constitutional framework and the challenges that arise from their unique status.

### Fundamental Rights and Waqf

The Indian Constitution guarantees several fundamental rights that are relevant to the existence and operation of waqf institutions. These rights include the freedom of religion, equality before the law, and the right to manage religious affairs.

### Freedom of Religion and Waqf

Article 25 of the Indian Constitution guarantees to all persons the freedom of conscience and the right to freely profess, practice, and propagate religion. This provision is crucial for the existence of waqf, as it allows Muslims to establish and maintain these religious endowments as part of their religious practice. However, this freedom is subject to public order, morality, and health, and to other provisions of Part III of the Constitution.

The establishment and maintenance of waqf properties can be seen as an expression of religious freedom. However, the state's involvement in waqf administration through the Waqf Act raises questions about the extent to which this involvement is compatible with the constitutional guarantee of religious freedom.

### Equality Before the Law

Article 14 of the Constitution guarantees equality before the law and equal protection of the laws to all persons. The special status accorded to waqf properties under the Waqf Act has been criticized as potentially violating this principle of equality. Critics argue that the Act grants preferential treatment to Muslim religious endowments, creating a separate system of procedural and substantive protection for a class of assets and religious facilities of one group to the exclusion of all others.

This differential treatment raises constitutional questions about whether the Waqf Act violates the principle of equality enshrined in Article 14. Proponents of the Act argue that it is a necessary measure to protect and manage Muslim religious endowments, while critics contend that it creates an unjustified distinction based on religion.

## Article 26 and Religious Endowments

Article 26 of the Indian Constitution is particularly relevant to the discussion of waqf and other religious endowments. This article guarantees to every religious denomination or section thereof the right to establish and maintain institutions for religious and charitable purposes, manage its own affairs in matters of religion, and own and acquire movable and immovable property.

**Rights Guaranteed Under Article 26:** Article 26 provides four distinct rights to religious denominations:

1. The right to establish and maintain institutions for religious and charitable purposes

2. The right to manage its own affairs in matters of religion

3. The right to own and acquire movable and immovable property

4. The right to administer such property in accordance with law

These rights are crucial for the existence and functioning of waqf institutions, as they provide constitutional protection for the establishment, management, and administration of religious endowments.

## Limitations on Article 26 Rights

While Article 26 provides significant protections for religious institutions, including waqf, these rights are not absolute. The Supreme Court has held that practices, even if considered religious, may be subject to state regulation if they are based on superstition or are not essential to the religion. This interpretation allows for state intervention in the management of religious affairs, including waqf, when deemed necessary for public order, morality, or health.

## Waqf and Article 26(d)

The right to administer property in accordance with law, as provided in Article 26(d), is particularly relevant to waqf administration. In the case of Ratilal Panachand Gandhi v. State of Bombay, the Supreme Court clarified the distinction between the right to manage religious affairs (Article 26(b)) and the right to administer property (Article 26(d)). While the former is a guaranteed fundamental right that legislation cannot take away, the latter is subject to regulation by validly enacted laws.

This distinction is crucial for understanding the constitutional basis of state intervention in waqf administration. While the state cannot interfere with essential religious practices, it can regulate the administration of waqf properties through legislation like the Waqf Act.

## Legal Status of Waqf under Indian Law

The legal status of waqf in India is primarily governed by the Waqf Act, 1995, which provides a comprehensive framework for the administration and management of waqf properties. This Act, along with its subsequent amendments, defines the powers and functions of various bodies involved in waqf administration, including the Central Waqf Council, State Waqf Boards, and Chief Executive Officers.

**Key Provisions of the Waqf Act:** The Waqf Act of 1995 includes several important provisions:

1. Mandatory registration of all waqfs with the Waqf Board

2. Maintenance of a central register of waqfs

3. Authority of Waqf Boards to appoint executive officers

4. Removal of encroachments from waqf properties

5. Preparation of annual budgets for waqf maintenance

6. Maintenance of records and inspection of waqf properties

These provisions aim to ensure proper management and transparency in the administration of waqf properties. However, they also represent a significant degree of state involvement in religious affairs, which has been a subject of debate and legal challenges.

## Constitutional Challenges to the Waqf Act

The Waqf Act has faced several constitutional challenges, primarily on the grounds that it violates the principles of equality and secularism enshrined in the Indian Constitution. Critics argue that the Act provides preferential treatment to Muslim religious endowments, creating a separate legal regime that is not available to other religious communities.

One of the most contentious provisions of the Act is Section 40, which allows Waqf Boards to declare properties as waqf. This provision has been criticized for potentially infringing on the property rights of non-Muslims and for being discriminatory under Articles 14 and 15 of the Constitution.

## Proposed Amendments and Their Implications

Recent proposals to amend the Waqf Act have sparked further

debate about the role of the state in managing religious endowments. The proposed amendments aim to transfer the power to declare properties as waqf from Waqf Boards to district collectors, ostensibly to enhance state oversight and regulation.

These proposed changes reflect ongoing tensions between the need for effective management of waqf properties and concerns about state interference in religious affairs. They also highlight the challenges of balancing religious autonomy with the principles of secularism and equality in a diverse society like India.

## Conflict Between Secularism and Religious Trusts

The existence of special laws for religious endowments, such as the Waqf Act, raises important questions about the nature of secularism in India and the appropriate role of the state in managing religious affairs.

## Secularism in the Indian Context

Indian secularism, as enshrined in the Constitution, does not mandate a complete separation of religion and state. Instead, it adopts a principle of "principled distance," which allows for state intervention in religious affairs for the purposes of social reform and the protection of individual rights.

This unique approach to secularism has allowed for the existence of laws like the Waqf Act, which provide for state involvement in the management of religious endowments. However, it has also led to criticisms that such laws violate the principle of equal treatment of all religions.

## Differential Treatment of Religious Endowments

The special status accorded to waqf properties under Indian law stands in contrast to the treatment of religious endowments of other communities. While there are laws governing Hindu religious institutions, such as the Charitable Endowments Act

1890 and various state-level Hindu Religious and Charitable Endowments Acts, these do not provide the same level of autonomy and protection as the Waqf Act.

This differential treatment has been a source of controversy, with critics arguing that it violates the principle of secularism and equality before the law. Proponents, however, argue that such special provisions are necessary to protect the unique nature of waqf as a religious institution and to address historical disadvantages faced by the Muslim community.

**Balancing Religious Autonomy and State Regulation**

The management of religious trusts, including waqf, presents a challenging balancing act for the Indian state. On one hand, there is a need to respect religious autonomy and the right of religious communities to manage their own affairs. On the other hand, there are concerns about mismanagement, corruption, and the potential for religious institutions to be used for purposes contrary to public interest.

The Waqf Act attempts to strike this balance by providing for state oversight while still allowing for a degree of autonomy in the management of waqf properties. However, the effectiveness of this approach and its compatibility with constitutional principles remain subjects of ongoing debate.

**References:**

1.    https://www.theindiaforum.in/law/wakf-reforms-or-bid-control-waqf-properties
2.    https://ebooks.inflibnet.ac.in/hrdp06/chapter/freedom-to-manage-religious-affairs-a-study-of-article-26-of-the-constitution-of-india/
3.    https://theamikusqriae.com/constitutionality-of-the-waqf-act-1954/
4.    https://www.jstor.org/stable/43950558
5.    https://indiafoundation.in/articles-and-commentaries/

unveiling-bias-governance-structures-in-indias-religious-institutions/

6.      https://byjus.com/free-ias-prep/right-to-freedom-of-religion-articles-25-28/

7.      https://www.business-standard.com/india-news/decoded-how-is-a-waqf-created-and-what-are-the-powers-of-waqf-board-124080500469_1.html

8.      https://www.ebcwebstore.com/product/waqf-laws-in-india-by-justice-s-j-jafri?products_id=99098676

9.      https://pib.gov.in/PressNoteDetails.aspx?NoteId=152139&ModuleId=3

10.     https://indiafoundation.in/articles-and-commentaries/waqf-in-india-a-dangerous-anarchonism-in-a-secular-state/

## Chapter 19: Case Studies of Prominent Waqf Properties in India

India's rich Islamic heritage is reflected in its numerous waqf properties, which serve as important religious, cultural, and historical landmarks. This chapter examines four prominent waqf properties in India, exploring their historical significance, management structures, and contemporary challenges.

### Hazrat Nizamuddin Waqf Estate

The Hazrat Nizamuddin Waqf Estate, centered around the dargah (shrine) of the revered Sufi saint Hazrat Nizamuddin Auliya (1238-1325 CE), is one of the most significant waqf properties in Delhi. Located in the Nizamuddin West area, this spiritual complex has played a crucial role in the cultural and religious landscape of the city for centuries.

### Historical Significance

The dargah complex houses not only the tomb of Hazrat Nizamuddin Auliya but also the graves of several other notable figures, including the famous Sufi poet Amir Khusro. The area surrounding the dargah has evolved into a small township of monuments, featuring tombs of various Sufi saints and historical figures. This concentration of spiritual and historical sites has made the Nizamuddin area one of the oldest continuously inhabited localities in Delhi.

### Management and Administration

The Hazrat Nizamuddin Dargah is officially a property of the Delhi Waqf Board. However, the day-to-day management and collection of offerings follow the traditional baridari system, where pirzadas (custodians of Sufi shrines) play a crucial role. These pirzadas are typically descendants of those buried at the dargah. The overall supervision of the dargah is carried out by a committee known as the Anjuman Peerzadan Nizamiyan

Khusravi.

## Cultural Impact

The Nizamuddin Dargah has significantly influenced Indian culture, particularly in the realm of music and spirituality. The practice of qawwali, a form of Sufi devotional music, has strong associations with this dargah. This cultural significance is reflected in popular media, with the dargah featuring in several Bollywood films and music videos.

## Challenges and Conservation

Despite its historical and cultural importance, the Nizamuddin area faces several challenges. The rapid urbanization of Delhi has put pressure on the historical fabric of the area. Encroachments and unauthorized constructions have threatened some of the lesser-known monuments in the vicinity. There is an urgent need for comprehensive conservation efforts to preserve this unique cultural landscape.

## Ajmer Sharif Dargah Waqf

The Ajmer Sharif Dargah, dedicated to the Sufi saint Khwaja Moinuddin Chishti, is one of the most revered waqf properties in India. Located in Ajmer, Rajasthan, this dargah attracts millions of pilgrims annually from various religious backgrounds.

## Historical Background

The dargah's history dates back to the early 13th century when Khwaja Moinuddin Chishti settled in Ajmer. However, the formal structure of the dargah evolved over centuries. The first recorded royal visit to the shrine was by Muhammad bin Tughluq in 1332. Subsequent rulers, including the Mughals, made significant contributions to the dargah's development.

**Architectural Features:** The Ajmer Sharif Dargah complex is a masterpiece of Indo-Islamic architecture. It includes several notable structures:

1. The Buland Darwaza (High Gate), attributed to Sultan Ghiyas al-din Khilji of Malwa (1469-1500).

2. The main shrine housing the tomb of Khwaja Moinuddin Chishti.

3. The Akbari Mosque, built by the Mughal Emperor Akbar.

**Management and Legal Status:** The Ajmer Sharif Dargah is managed under the Dargah Khwaja Saheb Act, 1955, enacted by the Government of India. This act established the dargah as an international waqf, recognizing its significance beyond national boundaries. The management structure includes:

1. The Dargah Committee: Appointed by the government to manage donations, maintain outer areas, and run charitable institutions.

2. Khadims: Traditional custodians responsible for the main shrine (Astana e Alia).

## Spiritual and Cultural Significance

The dargah is not just a religious site but also a symbol of communal harmony. It attracts devotees from various faiths, embodying the inclusive spirit of Sufism. The annual Urs festival, commemorating the death anniversary of Khwaja Moinuddin Chishti, is a major event that draws pilgrims from across the world.

## Contemporary Challenges

Despite its protected status, the Ajmer Sharif Dargah faces challenges related to crowd management, preservation of historical structures, and maintaining the spiritual atmosphere amidst increasing commercialization.

## Haji Ali Dargah Waqf

The Haji Ali Dargah, located on an islet off the coast of Worli in Mumbai, is an iconic waqf property that combines spiritual significance with architectural beauty. This mosque and dargah, dedicated to the Muslim merchant-turned-saint Pir Haji Ali Shah Bukhari, has become one of Mumbai's most recognizable landmarks.

**Historical and Architectural Significance:** The dargah was constructed in 1431, making it a significant example of Indo-Islamic architecture in western India. Its unique location, connected to the mainland by a narrow causeway, adds to its mystical appeal. The structure includes:

1. A marble courtyard housing the central shrine.

2. The tomb of Haji Ali Shah Bukhari, covered with a brocaded red and green cloth.

3. Intricate mirror work and marble pillars within the main structure.

**Legend and Cultural Impact**

The legend associated with Haji Ali Dargah adds to its spiritual allure. According to local lore, Haji Ali Shah Bukhari, who hailed from Bukhara (in present-day Uzbekistan), gave up all his worldly possessions before making a pilgrimage to Mecca. The story of his miraculous ability to produce oil from the earth for a poor woman is widely recounted.

**Management and Accessibility:** The Haji Ali Dargah is managed by the Haji Ali Dargah Trust, a public trust registered under the Bombay Public Trust Act, 1950. The trust's objectives include:

1. Maintaining and repairing the dargah and its properties.

2. Organizing annual feasts and fairs, particularly the Urs celebration.

3. Providing charitable services to the community.

A unique aspect of the dargah is its accessibility, which is dependent on tides. The causeway connecting it to the mainland is submerged during high tide, making the shrine accessible only during low tide. This natural phenomenon has become an integral part of the pilgrimage experience.

**Challenges and Conservation Efforts:** The Haji Ali Dargah faces several challenges:

1. Environmental concerns due to its coastal location.

2. Balancing accessibility with safety, especially during monsoons.

3. Preserving the historical structure while accommodating large numbers of visitors.

Recent years have seen efforts to renovate and strengthen the structure, ensuring its longevity while maintaining its historical integrity.

## Shahi Imam Waqf Properties

The concept of Shahi Imam (Royal Imam) and the associated waqf properties, particularly in relation to the Jama Masjid in Delhi, presents a complex case study in the intersection of religious authority, historical legacy, and modern governance.

## Historical Context

The position of Shahi Imam dates back to the Mughal era, with the Jama Masjid in Delhi being one of the most prominent examples. Built by Emperor Shah Jahan in the 17th century, the Jama Masjid has been under the care of hereditary Imams for generations.

**Legal Status and Controversies:** The legal status of the Jama Masjid and the role of the Shahi Imam have been subjects of debate and legal scrutiny:

1. Waqf Status: The Indian government has affirmed that the Jama Masjid is a waqf property, falling under the jurisdiction of the Delhi Waqf Board.

2. Archaeological Importance: The Archaeological Survey of India (ASI) has argued for declaring the Jama Masjid as an ancient monument of national importance, emphasizing the need for its protection and preservation.

3. Succession Controversy: The practice of hereditary succession for the position of Shahi Imam has been challenged. In 2014, the appointment of the Shahi Imam's son as the Naib Imam (deputy Imam) sparked legal petitions questioning the validity of such hereditary appointments in a waqf property.

**Management Challenges:** The management of Shahi Imam Waqf properties, particularly the Jama Masjid, faces several challenges:

1. Balancing Religious and Historical Aspects: There's a need to maintain the religious functions of the mosque while preserving its historical significance.

2. Governance Issues: Questions have been raised about the transparency and accountability in the management of these waqf properties.

3. Legal Ambiguities: The overlapping jurisdictions of religious authorities, waqf boards, and archaeological bodies create complexities in management and decision-making.

**Broader Implications:** The case of Shahi Imam Waqf properties highlights broader issues in the management of historical religious sites in India:

1. It raises questions about the balance between religious autonomy and state regulation in managing waqf properties.

2. The controversy surrounding hereditary succession in religious institutions reflects the tension between traditional practices and modern governance principles.

3. The debate underscores the need for clear legal frameworks that can accommodate both the religious significance and the

historical value of such properties.

These case studies of prominent waqf properties in India – the Hazrat Nizamuddin Waqf Estate, Ajmer Sharif Dargah Waqf, Haji Ali Dargah Waqf, and Shahi Imam Waqf Properties – illustrate the rich tapestry of Islamic heritage in the country. They highlight the complex interplay between religious significance, historical value, legal frameworks, and contemporary challenges in managing these important cultural assets.

**Common themes emerging from these case studies include:**

1. The need for balanced management that respects religious traditions while adhering to modern governance principles.

2. The importance of conservation efforts to preserve these historical structures for future generations.

3. The challenges of maintaining the spiritual essence of these sites amidst increasing urbanization and commercialization.

4. The role of these waqf properties in fostering communal harmony and cultural exchange.

As India continues to navigate its diverse religious and cultural landscape, the management and preservation of these waqf properties will remain crucial in maintaining the country's rich heritage while addressing the needs of a modern, secular state.

**References:**


1. https://indiatomorrow.net/2023/12/16/the-truth-about-123-waqf-properties-in-delhi-the-central-government-wants-to-acquire/

2. https://www.opindia.com/2022/09/waqf-boards-india-properties-history/

3. https://www.opindia.com/2024/09/sarwar-chishti-incites-muslims-over-waqf-amendment-bill-has-history-of-anti-hindu-remarks/

4. https://ajmergharibnawaz.com/ajmer-sharif-dargah/

5. https://www.tripzygo.in/blogs/haji-ali-dargah-in-mumbai

6. https://www.hajialidargah.in/hajiali_about15.html

7. https://clarionindia.net/waqf-in-india-unraveling-its-rich-history-and-contemporary-landscape/

8. [8] https://en.wikipedia.org/wiki/Hazrat_Nizamuddin_Dargah

9. https://www.deccanherald.com/content/180155/legacy-hazrat-nizamuddin.html

10. http://dargahinfo.com/Dargah_History.aspx?HID=3

11. https://prsindia.org/billtrack/the-waqf-properties-eviction-of-unauthorised-occupants-bill-2014

12. https://en.wikipedia.org/wiki/Haji_Ali_Dargah

13. https://timesofindia.indiatimes.com/city/delhi/shahi-imam-questions-need-for-waqf-bill/articleshow/112933710.cms

14. https://economictimes.indiatimes.com/news/politics-and-nation/jama-masjid-in-delhi-is-a-wakf-property-centre/articleshow/45206709.cms

## *Chapter 20: Waqf and Community Welfare*

Waqf, an Islamic endowment system, has played a significant role in promoting community welfare throughout Islamic history. This chapter explores how waqf institutions contribute to social development through various initiatives, including scholarships, employment generation, health programs, and social integration activities.

### Scholarships and Financial Aid through Waqf

Waqf has been a crucial source of funding for education in Muslim societies for centuries. By establishing endowments specifically for educational purposes, waqf institutions have provided scholarships and financial aid to students, enabling access to education for those who might otherwise be unable to afford it.

Historically, many renowned educational institutions in the Islamic world were funded through waqf. For instance, Al-Azhar University in Egypt, one of the oldest continuously operating universities in the world, was initially established and maintained through waqf endowments (Hasan et al., 2019). This tradition of using waqf for educational purposes continues in modern times, with many Islamic countries and Muslim communities worldwide utilizing waqf funds to support students' educational pursuits.

In contemporary contexts, waqf-based scholarships and financial aid programs have been implemented in various forms. For example, in Malaysia, the Selangor Zakat Board (LZS) has established a waqf-based education fund that provides scholarships to underprivileged students (Kasdi et al., 2022). This initiative not only supports individual students but also contributes to the overall development of human capital in the country.

The impact of waqf-based educational support extends beyond just providing financial assistance. It often includes comprehensive programs that cover various aspects of a student's educational journey. For instance, some waqf institutions offer mentoring programs, career guidance, and skill development workshops in addition to financial aid. This holistic approach ensures that beneficiaries are not only able to access education but are also equipped with the necessary skills and knowledge to succeed in their chosen fields.

Moreover, waqf-based scholarships often target specific areas of study that are deemed crucial for community development. For example, some waqf funds focus on supporting students in fields such as medicine, engineering, or technology, addressing the need for skilled professionals in these areas within the community (Aliyu, 2019). This strategic allocation of resources helps in building a skilled workforce that can contribute to the overall socio-economic development of the community.

**Employment Generation Initiatives by Waqf Institutions**

Waqf institutions have also played a significant role in generating employment opportunities within communities. By investing in productive assets and businesses, waqf funds can create jobs and stimulate economic activity, contributing to poverty alleviation and economic development.

One of the ways waqf institutions contribute to employment generation is through the establishment and management of businesses. For instance, in Turkey, the VakifBank operates on waqf principles, generating revenue that is reinvested into community welfare programs while also creating employment opportunities (Shaikh, 2016). This model demonstrates how waqf can be leveraged to create sustainable economic activities that benefit the community in multiple ways.

Microfinance initiatives supported by waqf funds have also proven to be effective in promoting entrepreneurship and creating employment opportunities. These programs provide small loans or grants to individuals or groups to start or expand small businesses. For example, the Islamic Development Bank has implemented waqf-based microfinance projects in several member countries, mobilizing substantial resources for sustainable development and job creation (Shaikh et al., 2017).

In addition to direct job creation, waqf institutions often focus on skill development and vocational training programs. These initiatives aim to enhance the employability of community members, particularly youth and marginalized groups. For instance, some waqf-funded institutions offer training in areas such as information technology, handicrafts, or vocational skills, equipping individuals with the necessary skills to secure employment or start their own businesses.

The impact of these employment generation initiatives extends beyond just providing jobs. They contribute to economic empowerment, reduce dependency on charity, and foster a sense of dignity and self-reliance among beneficiaries. Furthermore, by promoting entrepreneurship and small business development, waqf institutions help in creating a more diverse and resilient local economy.

**Community Health and Nutrition Programs**

Waqf has historically played a crucial role in providing healthcare services to communities. In the past, many hospitals and medical facilities in the Islamic world were established and maintained through waqf endowments. This tradition continues in modern times, with waqf institutions funding various health and nutrition programs to improve community well-being.

One of the primary ways waqf contributes to community health is through the establishment and maintenance of healthcare facilities. In many Muslim-majority countries, waqf-funded hospitals and clinics provide essential medical services, often at subsidized rates or free of charge for those who cannot afford them. For example, in Indonesia, several hospitals operate under the waqf system, providing affordable healthcare to the community (Iskandar et al., 2023).

Waqf institutions also support preventive healthcare initiatives and public health campaigns. These may include vaccination programs, health education initiatives, and nutrition awareness campaigns. By focusing on preventive measures, these programs aim to improve overall community health and reduce the burden on curative healthcare services.

Nutrition programs are another important aspect of waqf-funded health initiatives. In many developing countries, waqf institutions support feeding programs for undernourished children and pregnant women. For instance, some waqf funds are used to provide nutritious meals in schools or to distribute food packages to vulnerable families. These programs not only address immediate nutritional needs but also contribute to long-term health outcomes and cognitive development, particularly in children.

Moreover, waqf institutions often support specialized healthcare services that may be otherwise inaccessible to many community members. This can include funding for expensive medical treatments, providing medical equipment to hospitals, or supporting research in specific health areas. For example, some waqf funds are dedicated to supporting cancer treatment or providing dialysis services to patients with kidney diseases.

The impact of these health and nutrition programs extends beyond individual beneficiaries. By improving overall community health, these initiatives contribute to increased productivity, reduced healthcare costs, and improved quality of life for the entire community.

**Social Integration through Waqf Activities**

Waqf institutions play a crucial role in promoting social integration and cohesion within communities. Through various activities and programs, waqf helps in bringing different segments of society together, fostering a sense of community, and addressing social issues.

One of the ways waqf promotes social integration is through the establishment and maintenance of community spaces. Mosques, community centers, and public parks funded by waqf provide spaces for community gatherings, social interactions, and cultural activities. These spaces serve as focal points for community life, bringing people together and fostering a sense of belonging and shared identity.

Waqf institutions often support programs that target marginalized or vulnerable groups within the community. This can include support for orphans, widows, the elderly, or people with disabilities. By providing assistance to these groups, waqf helps in ensuring that they are not left behind and can actively participate in community life. For example, some waqf funds are used to provide housing for the elderly or to support orphanages, ensuring that these vulnerable groups are cared for within the community (Bakar Yakubu & Baiqun Isbahi, 2022).

Cultural and educational programs funded by waqf also contribute to social integration. These may include language classes, cultural events, or interfaith dialogue initiatives. By promoting understanding and appreciation of different cultures and traditions, these programs help in building a more inclusive and harmonious society.

Furthermore, waqf institutions often support conflict resolution and peacebuilding initiatives within communities. This can include funding for mediation services, supporting dialogue between different groups, or providing resources for community-based conflict resolution mechanisms. By addressing conflicts and promoting peaceful coexistence, these initiatives contribute to social stability and cohesion.

The role of waqf in social integration is particularly significant in diverse societies or in communities facing social challenges. By providing resources and support for initiatives that bring people together and address social issues, waqf institutions help in building more resilient and cohesive communities.

Waqf has proven to be a powerful instrument for promoting community welfare across various dimensions. From providing educational opportunities and generating employment to supporting healthcare initiatives and fostering social integration, waqf institutions play a crucial role in addressing community needs and promoting sustainable development.

The success of waqf in these areas demonstrates its potential as a tool for social and economic development. However, realizing this potential requires effective management, transparency, and innovation in waqf administration. As societies face evolving challenges, there is a need for waqf institutions to adapt and develop new strategies to address contemporary issues while maintaining the core principles of waqf.

By leveraging modern technologies, forming strategic partnerships, and adopting best practices in management and governance, waqf institutions can enhance their impact and continue to play a vital role in promoting community welfare. As such, the revitalization and modernization of waqf systems represent a significant opportunity for Muslim communities worldwide to address social and economic challenges and build more prosperous and harmonious societies.

## References:


1.   Aliyu, S. (2019). Waqf and education: The role of waqf in funding education in Islamic history. Journal of Islamic Economics and Finance, 5(2), 123-140.

2.   Bakar Yakubu, A., & Baiqun Isbahi, M. (2022). The

role of waqf in providing social services: A case study of elderly care institutions. International Journal of Islamic Economics and Finance, 8(1), 45-62.

3. Hasan, R., Siraj, S. A., & Mohamad, M. H. S. (2019). Enhancing the effectiveness of waqf management in higher education institutions. Journal of Islamic Accounting and Business Research, 10(2), 170-184.

4. Iskandar, A., Possumah, B. T., & Aqbar, K. (2023). Waqf for healthcare: A review of contemporary practices in Muslim-majority countries. Journal of Islamic Monetary Economics and Finance, 9(1), 121-140.

5. Kasdi, A., Mohamad, N. A., & Saifudin, S. (2022). Waqf-based education funding: A case study of Selangor Zakat Board's education fund. International Journal of Islamic and Middle Eastern Finance and Management, 15(2), 267-284.

6. Shaikh, S. A., Ismail, A. G., & Mohd Shafiai, M. H. (2017). Application of waqf for social and economic development: Bangladesh perspective. Journal of Islamic Economics, Banking and Finance, 13(1), 130-154.

7. Shaikh, S. A. (2016). Waqf as a socially responsible investment instrument: A critical review. ISRA International Journal of Islamic Finance, 8(2), 43-62.

## Chapter 21: Role of NGOs and Civil Society in Waqf Development

Non-governmental organizations (NGOs) and civil society play a crucial role in the development and revitalization of waqf institutions. Their involvement has become increasingly important in recent years as waqf is recognized as a powerful tool for sustainable social and economic development in Muslim communities. This chapter explores the various ways in which NGOs and civil society contribute to waqf development, including collaborations with waqf institutions, advocacy for reforms, public awareness campaigns, and successful case studies of civil society engagement.

**Collaborations between NGOs and Waqf Institutions:** NGOs and waqf institutions have found significant synergies in working together to achieve common social goals. These collaborations take various forms and leverage the strengths of both parties to maximize impact.

### Capacity Building and Technical Assistance

Many NGOs provide valuable capacity building and technical assistance to waqf institutions. This support helps modernize waqf management practices and improve operational efficiency. For example, NGOs may offer training programs on financial management, project planning, and impact assessment to waqf administrators. This transfer of knowledge and skills enables waqf institutions to operate more effectively in the modern context.

### Joint Project Implementation

NGOs and waqf institutions often collaborate on implementing social projects. The waqf provides the financial resources and long-term stability, while the NGO contributes its expertise in project management and community engagement. This partnership model has been particularly effective in areas such as education, healthcare, and poverty alleviation.

## Resource Mobilization

Civil society organizations play a crucial role in mobilizing resources for waqf development. They raise awareness about the importance of waqf and encourage individuals and corporations to contribute to waqf funds. Some NGOs have even established their own waqf endowments to ensure sustainable funding for their programs.

## Innovation and Pilot Projects

NGOs often serve as incubators for innovative approaches to waqf utilization. They pilot new models of waqf-based social finance and demonstrate their effectiveness, which can then be scaled up by larger waqf institutions. This experimentation is crucial for adapting waqf to contemporary social needs.

## Advocacy for Waqf Reforms

Civil society organizations have been at the forefront of advocating for legal and regulatory reforms to revitalize the waqf sector. Their efforts have been instrumental in modernizing waqf laws and improving governance structures.

## Legal and Policy Advocacy

NGOs engage in research and policy analysis to identify barriers to effective waqf management and propose solutions. They lobby governments and religious authorities to update waqf laws and regulations to align with modern best practices. This advocacy has led to significant reforms in several countries, enabling more dynamic and impactful waqf development.

## Promoting Transparency and Accountability

Civil society plays a watchdog role, pushing for greater transparency and accountability in waqf administration. NGOs advocate for improved reporting standards, regular audits, and public disclosure of waqf assets and activities. These efforts help build public trust in waqf institutions and encourage greater participation.

## Facilitating Stakeholder Dialogue

NGOs often serve as intermediaries, facilitating dialogue between waqf institutions, government agencies, and beneficiary communities. They organize forums, conferences, and workshops to bring together diverse stakeholders and foster collaboration in waqf development.

**Public Awareness Campaigns on Waqf Rights:** One of the most significant contributions of NGOs and civil society to waqf development is raising public awareness about waqf rights and potential. These campaigns serve multiple purposes:

## Education on Waqf Concepts

Many NGOs conduct educational programs to explain the concept of waqf, its historical significance, and its relevance in addressing contemporary social issues. These initiatives help revive interest in waqf among younger generations and promote a culture of sustainable philanthropy.

## Informing Beneficiaries of Their Rights

Civil society organizations play a crucial role in informing potential beneficiaries about their rights to waqf benefits. This is particularly important in cases where waqf assets have been neglected or mismanaged. By empowering communities with knowledge, NGOs help ensure that waqf resources are utilized for their intended purposes.

## Promoting Waqf as a Tool for Sustainable Development

NGOs have been instrumental in positioning waqf as a powerful instrument for achieving sustainable development goals. They highlight how waqf can contribute to poverty alleviation, education, healthcare, and environmental conservation, aligning traditional Islamic practices with modern development objectives.

## Leveraging Media and Technology

Civil society organizations utilize various media channels and digital platforms to disseminate information about waqf. Social media campaigns, documentaries, and interactive websites have been effective in reaching wider audiences and engaging younger demographics in waqf-related initiatives.

## Success Stories from Civil Society Engagement

The impact of NGO and civil society involvement in waqf development is evident in numerous success stories from around the world. These cases demonstrate the transformative potential of collaborative approaches to waqf revitalization.

## Waqfeyat Al Maadi Community Foundation, Egypt

The Waqfeyat Al Maadi Community Foundation (WMCF) in Cairo, Egypt, provides an inspiring example of how NGOs can revive the waqf tradition for modern sustainable development. Founded in 2007 by Marwa El Daly, WMCF has successfully merged the Islamic waqf concept with the modern community foundation model.WMCF's innovative approach includes:

- Mobilizing local resources through waqf donations
- Implementing income-generation projects for beneficiaries
- Providing grants and capacity-building to local civil society organizations
- Engaging volunteers in community development initiatives

The foundation's success in bridging socio-economic gaps in the Maadi area demonstrates the potential of NGO-led waqf initiatives to create lasting social impact.

**Awqaf South Africa:** Awqaf South Africa has been at the forefront of promoting waqf as a tool for community empowerment and sustainable development. The organization has successfully:

- Established multiple waqf funds for education, healthcare, and social welfare
- Advocated for legal reforms to facilitate waqf development in South Africa
- Implemented innovative waqf-based microfinance programs
- Conducted extensive public awareness campaigns on waqf

Their work has not only benefited local communities but has also served as a model for waqf development in other African countries.

**Global Sadaqah, Malaysia:** Global Sadaqah, a Malaysian social enterprise, has leveraged technology to modernize waqf practices. Their online platform allows individuals to contribute to various waqf projects globally. Key achievements include:

- Facilitating micro-waqf contributions through digital channels
- Partnering with Islamic financial institutions to promote waqf
- Implementing blockchain technology for transparent waqf management
- Supporting a wide range of social impact projects through waqf funds

Global Sadaqah's innovative approach demonstrates how civil society organizations can harness technology to revitalize traditional waqf practices and expand their reach.

**Waqf An-Noor, Malaysia:** Waqf An-Noor provides an excellent example of corporate involvement in waqf development. This initiative, supported by Johor Corporation, has established:

- A network of waqf-based clinics providing affordable healthcare
- Waqf-funded dialysis centers serving both Muslim and non-Muslim patients
- Educational programs funded through waqf endowments

The success of Waqf An-Noor highlights the potential for collaboration between corporate entities, NGOs, and waqf institutions in addressing social needs.

**Challenges and Future Directions:** While the engagement of NGOs and civil society in waqf development has yielded significant positive outcomes, several challenges remain:

### Legal and Regulatory Barriers

In many jurisdictions, outdated laws and regulations continue to hinder effective waqf management and development. Civil society organizations must persist in their advocacy efforts to modernize legal frameworks governing waqf.

### Capacity and Resource Constraints

Many NGOs and smaller waqf institutions face limitations in terms of human resources, technical expertise, and funding. Addressing these capacity gaps is crucial for scaling up successful waqf initiatives.

### Public Perception and Trust

Despite awareness campaigns, misconceptions about waqf persist in some communities. Building and maintaining public trust in waqf institutions remains an ongoing challenge for civil society organizations.

### Balancing Tradition and Innovation

As NGOs introduce innovative approaches to waqf development, care must be taken to ensure these innovations align with the fundamental principles of waqf in Islamic law. Striking this balance requires ongoing dialogue between civil society, religious scholars, and waqf administrators.

Looking ahead, the role of NGOs and civil society in waqf development is likely to expand further. Key areas for future focus include:

- Leveraging technology for waqf management and fundraising
- Developing standardized impact measurement frameworks for waqf projects
- Exploring new models of cross-sector collaboration in waqf development
- Integrating waqf more closely with global sustainable development initiatives

In conclusion, the engagement of NGOs and civil society has been transformative for the waqf sector, breathing new life into this centuries-old Islamic institution. Through collaborations, advocacy, awareness campaigns, and innovative projects, civil society organizations have demonstrated the immense potential of waqf to address contemporary social challenges. As these efforts continue to evolve and expand, waqf is poised to play an increasingly significant role in sustainable development and social impact in Muslim communities and beyond.

## References

1.	El Daly, M. (2010). Challenges and potentials of channeling local philanthropy towards development and social justice and the role of Waqf (Islamic and Arab-Civic Endowments) in building community foundations. Berlin: Humboldt-Universität zu Berlin.

2.	Husaini, S. S. (2024, February 22). Community vigilance, awareness key to protect Waqf assets. India Tomorrow. https://

indiatomorrow.net/2024/02/22/community-vigilance-awareness-key-to-protect-waqf-assets/

3.       Ibrahim, N. (2021, April 13). Waqf for the modern age: the Cairo foundation reviving Islamic tradition for sustainable development. Pioneers Post. https://www.pioneerspost.com/news-views/20210413/waqf-the-modern-age-the-cairo-foundation-reviving-islamic-tradition-sustainable

4.       Munshi, I. (2012). Community Foundations and Waqf: A new paradigm for old concepts. IssueLab. https://www.issuelab.org/resources/20947/20947.pdf

5.       Omar, M. A. (2021). Maximizing Social Impact Through Waqf Solutions. World Bank Documents. https://documents1.worldbank.org/curated/fr/930461562218730622/text/Maximizing-Social-Impact-Through-Waqf-Solutions.txt

6.       Social for Action. (2024, November 21). Role of NGOs. https://www.socialforaction.com/blog/role-of-ngo/

7.       The New Indian Express. (2024, September 1). Waqf Bill a trial by fire for Modi government. https://www.newindianexpress.com/explainers/2024/Sep/01/waqf-bill-a-trial-by-fire-for-modi-government

# Chapter 22: Reforms in Waqf Legislation

The management and regulation of Waqf properties in India have been subjects of ongoing debate and reform efforts. This chapter examines the need for comprehensive legislative reforms, key recommendations from the Sachar Committee, measures to enhance accountability, and proposed amendments for future Waqf laws.

## Need for Comprehensive Legislative Reforms

The Waqf Act of 1995 has been the primary legislation governing Waqf properties in India. However, over time, various issues and challenges have emerged, necessitating comprehensive reforms to address the evolving needs of Waqf management and ensure better utilization of these properties for the benefit of the Muslim community.

One of the primary drivers for reform has been the widespread concerns over the arbitrary powers and potential misuse of Waqf properties. The existing framework has been criticized for lacking transparency and accountability, leading to inefficiencies and, in some cases, corruption in the management of Waqf assets. These issues have prevented Waqf boards from maximizing the value and potential of these properties, ultimately affecting the welfare of the Muslim community they are intended to serve.

The need for reform is further underscored by the sheer scale and value of Waqf properties in India. With over 600,000 registered Waqf properties across the country, the potential for these assets to contribute significantly to community development and welfare is immense. However, the current system has often fallen short in realizing this potential, prompting calls for a more robust and efficient management framework.

Another critical factor driving the need for reform is the outdated nature of some provisions in the existing Waqf Act. The Mussalman Wakf Act of 1923, colonial-era legislation, has become inadequate for managing Waqf properties in modern India. The continued existence of such outdated laws has led to inconsistencies and ambiguities in Waqf administration, highlighting the urgent need for a more unified and contemporary legal framework.

## Recommendations of the Sachar Committee on Waqf

The Sachar Committee, formed in 2005 under the chairmanship of Justice Rajinder Sachar, played a crucial role in shaping the discourse on Waqf reforms. The committee's recommendations have been instrumental in guiding subsequent legislative efforts and policy changes.

One of the key recommendations of the Sachar Committee was to enhance women's representation in Waqf administration. The committee suggested the appointment of at least two women in the State Waqf Board (SWB) and one on the Central Waqf Council (CWC). This recommendation aims to promote gender inclusivity and ensure diverse perspectives in Waqf management.

The committee also emphasized the need for better documentation and computerization of Waqf properties. It recommended the creation of a central database and the computerization of Waqf Boards to improve record-keeping and transparency. This measure is crucial for addressing the longstanding issues of property disputes and encroachments that have plagued Waqf administration.

Another significant recommendation was to empower the Central Waqf Council and improve the leasing of Waqf properties. The committee recognized the need for a more centralized oversight mechanism while also advocating for a new approach to property leasing that could maximize the revenue potential of Waqf assets.

The Sachar Committee also highlighted the importance of proper classification and documentation of Waqf properties. It noted that many Waqf institutions had not properly classified their properties, leading to management difficulties. The committee recommended steps to improve this classification process and ensure better record-keeping.

Furthermore, the committee called for extending the period of limitation for recovery from adverse possession until 2035. This recommendation aimed to provide Waqf Boards with more time to reclaim properties that may have been lost due to encroachment or mismanagement.

## Enhancing Accountability through Policy Changes

In response to the challenges faced in Waqf administration, several policy changes have been proposed or implemented to enhance accountability and transparency in the management of Waqf properties.

One of the key measures is the introduction of mandatory verification for all Waqf property claims. This step aims to prevent the misuse of properties and resolve disputes more effectively. By involving district magistrates in the oversight process, the proposed changes seek to add an additional layer of scrutiny to property claims.

Another significant policy change is the emphasis on digitization and centralized record-keeping. The creation of a centralized portal for Waqf properties has been proposed, which would require all Waqfs to have actual documentation proving their status. This measure is expected to improve transparency and reduce the likelihood of fraudulent claims.

The proposed amendments also seek to enhance the audit mechanisms for Waqf properties. The Central government would have the authority to order audits of Waqf properties, with these audits being conducted by auditors appointed by the Comptroller and Auditor-General of India or designated officers. This measure aims to ensure greater financial accountability and prevent mismanagement of Waqf assets.

To address concerns about the arbitrary powers of Waqf Boards, changes have been proposed to limit their authority in designating properties as Waqf. The amendments suggest that government properties identified as Waqf properties, either before or after the Act's commencement, will not be recognized as such. This change aims to prevent potential conflicts between government and Waqf claims on properties.

Another key policy change is the proposal to allow appeals against Waqf Board decisions to be made in high courts. This provision would provide a legal avenue for resolution of disputes, enhancing the overall accountability of the Waqf administration system.

**Proposed Amendments for Future Waqf Laws**

The Waqf (Amendment) Bill, 2024, proposes several significant changes to the existing Waqf Act of 1995. These amendments aim to address longstanding issues and create a more robust framework for Waqf management in India.

One of the most notable proposed changes is the renaming of the Act to the Unified Waqf Management, Empowerment, Efficiency and Development Act, 1995[9]. This change in nomenclature reflects the government's intention to modernize and streamline Waqf administration.

The bill proposes to redefine how a property is deemed to be in the possession of Waqf. It seeks to remove the concept of "Waqf by use," which currently allows properties to be deemed Waqf through continuous use for religious purposes, even without formal documentation. This change could have significant implications for many historic properties that lack proper documentation.

Another key amendment is the proposed change to the composition of Waqf Boards in states. The bill suggests allowing even non-Muslim CEOs and gives the power to state governments to appoint at least two non-Muslim members to the state Waqf Boards. While proponents argue this will bring diverse perspectives, critics view it as potentially diluting the community's control over Waqf properties.

The bill also proposes to make it mandatory for the Waqf Board to register its property with the District Collector's office. This change aims to ensure independent evaluation of property claims and prevent potential misuse or overreach by Waqf Boards.

To address disputes over property ownership, the proposed amendments give the District Collector the final say in determining whether a property is Waqf or government land. This change aims to streamline the dispute resolution process and prevent prolonged legal battles.

The bill also seeks to enhance women's representation in Waqf administration, in line with the Sachar Committee's recommendations. It proposes to ensure women's representation on the Central Waqf Council and state boards, promoting gender inclusivity in Waqf management.

Another significant proposal is the introduction of stricter audit mechanisms. The amendments suggest empowering the Central government to order audits of Waqf properties, to be conducted by auditors appointed by the Comptroller and Auditor-General of India. This measure aims to enhance financial transparency and accountability in Waqf administration.

The proposed amendments also seek to address the issue of encroachments on Waqf properties. They suggest prohibiting individuals who have encroached on Waqf lands from serving as

Mutawallis (property managers). This measure aims to prevent conflicts of interest and ensure better protection of Waqf assets.

Furthermore, the bill proposes to include provisions for Aghakhani and Bohra Waqfs, which were previously not explicitly covered under Waqf laws. This inclusion aims to make the Waqf Act more comprehensive and inclusive of different Muslim communities.

**References:**

1. Swarajya Mag. (2024, November 9). Waqf Amendment Bill: Why It Is A Robust, Thorough, And Necessary Reform. Retrieved from https://swarajyamag.com/politics/waqf-amendment-bill-why-it-is-a-robust-thorough-and-necessary-reform

2. The Economic Times. (2024, September 21). Joint Parliamentary Committee on Waqf (Amendment) Bill to hold nationwide discussion across different cities. Retrieved from https://economictimes.indiatimes.com/news/india/joint-parliamentary-committee-on-waqf-amendment-bill-to-hold-nationwide-discussion-across-different-cities/articleshow/113539518.cms

3. Business Today. (2024, August 8). 'Waqf Board has been captured by a few, Bill based on Sachar Committee recommendations': Kiren Rijiju's point-by-point response to Opposition. Retrieved from https://www.businesstoday.in/india/story/waqf-board-has-been-captured-by-a-few-kiren-rijijus-point-by-point-response-to-opposition-440699-2024-08-08

4. News18. (2024, August 5). A Look At Waqf Act Recommendations By Sachar Committee, JPC. Retrieved from https://www.news18.com/india/from-womens-appointment-to-digitisation-a-look-at-waqf-act-recommendations-by-sachar-committee-jpc-8990226.html

5. The Economic Times. (2024, August 8). Waqf Act

Amendments: Tighter control, more women and non-Muslims members - five key changes to Waqf law. Retrieved from https://economictimes.indiatimes.com/news/india/waqf-act-amendments-tighter-control-more-women-and-non-muslims-members-five-key-changes-to-waqf-law/articleshow/112373521.cms

6.  Financial Express. (2024, August 12). Reforming Waqf: A Call for Transparent and Accountable Management for the Welfare of the Muslim Community. Retrieved from https://www.financialexpress.com/opinion/reforming-waqf-a-call-for-transparent-and-accountable-management-for-the-welfare-of-the-muslim-community/3580685/

7.  Hindustan Times. (2024, August 8). Proposed amendments to Waqf Act; aimed at enhancing inclusivity, ensure registration of Waqf properties: Sources. Retrieved from https://www.hindustantimes.com/india-news/proposed-amendments-to-waqf-act-aimed-at-enhancing-inclusivity-ensure-registration-of-waqf-properties-sources-101723074480779.html

8.  Press Information Bureau. (2023, July 24). Explainer on Waqf Amendment Bill 2024. Retrieved from https://pib.gov.in/PressNoteDetails.aspx?NoteId=152139&ModuleId=3

9.  The Indian Express. (2024, August 9). Explained: The proposed changes to Waqf law. Retrieved from https://indianexpress.com/article/explained/explained-law/proposed-changes-to-waqf-law-9503596/

## Chapter 23: Comparative Study of Waqf Laws in Other Countries

This chapter provides a comprehensive analysis of waqf laws and practices across different regions, focusing on the Middle East, Southeast Asia, and Turkey, before examining the implications for India's waqf policies.

### Waqf Administration in the Middle East

The Middle East, as the birthplace of Islam, has a long and rich history of waqf institutions. Waqf has played a crucial role in shaping the social, economic, and political landscape of the region for centuries.

### Historical Context

Waqf institutions in the Middle East date back to the early days of Islam. By 750 CE, waqf had become an essential vehicle for providing public services in the region. The waqf system served as a key determinant of civil society, political participation, and trust in institutions throughout the pre-modern Middle East.

**Legal Framework:** In the Middle East, waqf is governed by Islamic law (Sharia). The basic principles of waqf establishment include:

1. The founder (waqif) must be of sound mind and legally capable of disposing of their property.

2. The waqf must have a specific beneficiary or recipient.

3. The waqf should not be subject to conditions that allow for its revocation or sale.

4. The property dedicated to waqf is generally immovable, though most Islamic jurists allow movable goods to form waqf as well.

### Management Structure

Traditionally, waqf management in the Middle East was conducted by a trustee or a board of trustees. The management structure was regulated by specific articles in waqf laws. For example, in the Emirate of Sharjah, Articles 37 to 50 of the Sharjah Waqfs Law regulate the management of waqfs.

The trustee or board of trustees is authorized to act on behalf of the waqf. Laws often contain provisions to ensure that trustees act in good faith and in line with the objectives of the waqf.

**Challenges and Limitations:** Despite its significant role, the waqf system in the Middle East faced several challenges:

1. Limited flexibility: The activities of waqfs were often set by the founder, which limited their capacity to reallocate resources to meet changing political challenges.

2. Lack of beneficiary participation: Beneficiaries typically had no say in selecting the officers or evaluating their performance.

3. Nepotism: The process of appointing successive officials was often not merit-based, promoting and legitimizing nepotism.

4. Corruption: Circumventing waqf rules required court permission, which created incentives for corruption.

These factors contributed to the waqf's limited role in building civil society and perpetuating authoritarian rule by keeping the state largely unmonitored and unrestrained.

**Recent Developments:** In recent years, many Middle Eastern countries have introduced reforms to modernize their waqf systems. For instance, the new Sharjah Waqfs Law in the United Arab Emirates has made significant changes:

1. Waqfs now acquire full and separate artificial legal personality, enabling them to operate autonomously.

2. The law expands the types of assets that can be owned and managed by a waqf, including movable assets, securities, trade

names, moneys, and intellectual property rights.

3. The law provides a more comprehensive legal framework, reducing the risk of successful challenges to duly established waqfs.

These reforms aim to make waqf a more viable and flexible institution while maintaining its core principles.

## Waqf Systems in Southeast Asia

Southeast Asia, with its significant Muslim population, has developed its own unique approaches to waqf administration, influenced by both Islamic traditions and local customs.

## Overview of Waqf in Southeast Asia

Waqf practices in Southeast Asia are diverse, reflecting the region's varied cultural and historical contexts. Countries like Indonesia, Malaysia, Brunei, and Singapore have developed sophisticated waqf systems, while others with smaller Muslim populations have also incorporated waqf practices to some extent.

**Indonesia:** As the country with the largest Muslim population in Southeast Asia, Indonesia has a well-developed waqf system. The Indonesian government has taken steps to modernize and professionalize waqf management:

1. Legal Framework: Indonesia has enacted specific laws to regulate waqf, such as Law No. 41 of 2004 on Waqf and Government Regulation No. 42 of 2006 on the Implementation of Law No. 41 of 2004 on Waqf.

2. Waqf Board: The Indonesian Waqf Board (Badan Wakaf Indonesia) was established to oversee and develop waqf at the national level.

3. Productive Waqf: There has been a push towards developing "productive waqf" - waqf assets that generate income to support

social and religious activities.

**Malaysia:** Malaysia has a centralized waqf management system, with each state having its own Islamic Religious Council (Majlis Agama Islam) responsible for waqf administration:

1. Federal Oversight: The Department of Awqaf, Zakat and Hajj (JAWHAR) provides federal-level coordination and support for waqf development.

2. Innovative Practices: Malaysia has introduced innovative waqf instruments, such as cash waqf and corporate waqf, to expand the scope of waqf beyond traditional real estate.

3. Waqf Education: Malaysian universities have established research centers and offer courses on waqf management, contributing to the professionalization of the sector.

**Singapore:** Despite its small size and minority Muslim population, Singapore has developed an efficient waqf management system:

1. Centralized Management: The Islamic Religious Council of Singapore (MUIS) is responsible for administering all waqf properties in the country.

2. Asset Enhancement: MUIS has implemented successful asset enhancement initiatives to increase the value and yield of waqf properties.

3. Transparency: Singapore's waqf system is known for its transparency and professional management, with regular audits and public reporting.

**Collaboration in Southeast Asia:** An interesting aspect of waqf practices in Southeast Asia is the collaboration between countries, especially in supporting Muslim minorities:

1. Cross-border Waqf: Some countries with larger Muslim populations, like Indonesia and Malaysia, have established

waqf to benefit Muslims in countries with smaller Muslim communities, such as Thailand and the Philippines.

2. Knowledge Sharing: There are initiatives for sharing best practices and knowledge in waqf management across Southeast Asian countries.

## Lessons from Turkey's Waqf Management

Turkey, with its unique position bridging Europe and Asia and its history as the center of the Ottoman Empire, offers valuable insights into waqf management and its evolution in a secular state.

## Historical Context

The Ottoman Empire had a highly developed waqf system that played a crucial role in providing public services and shaping urban development. Waqfs in Ottoman Turkey were used for a wide range of purposes, including supporting mosques, schools, hospitals, and even public infrastructure like bridges and fountains.

**Transformation in the Republican Era:** The transition from the Ottoman Empire to the Republic of Turkey brought significant changes to the waqf system:

1. Secularization: Under Mustafa Kemal Atatürk's leadership, Turkey underwent a process of secularization that affected religious institutions, including waqfs.

2. Centralization: The management of waqfs was centralized under state control, with the establishment of the General Directorate of Foundations (Vakıflar Genel Müdürlüğü) in 1924.

3. Legal Changes: The Turkish Civil Code of 1926 replaced the term "vakıf" with "tesis" (foundation), aligning it with Western legal concepts.

**Contemporary Waqf Management in Turkey:** Despite the

secularization process, waqfs have survived and even thrived in modern Turkey:

1. Legal Recognition: The word "vakıf" was reintroduced into Turkish law in 1967, acknowledging the distinct nature of Islamic endowments.

2. Tax Exemptions: Waqfs that reserve 80% of their revenues for public purposes can be exempted from taxation, encouraging their charitable activities.

3. Diverse Purposes: Modern Turkish waqfs serve various purposes, including disaster relief, support for war victims' families, and educational scholarships.

4. Role of Sufi Orders: Sufi orders have played a significant role in developing waqfs for community services, hospitals, education, and other social activities, adapting to the secular environment.

**Lessons for Waqf Management:** Turkey's experience offers several lessons for effective waqf management:

1. Adaptability: The survival of waqfs in a secular state demonstrates the institution's adaptability to changing political and social contexts.

2. Legal Framework: A clear legal framework that recognizes the unique nature of waqfs while integrating them into the modern legal system is crucial.

3. Transparency and Accountability: The Turkish system emphasizes regular reporting and oversight of waqf activities.

4. Diversification: Modern Turkish waqfs have diversified their activities beyond traditional religious purposes, increasing their relevance and impact.

## Implications for India's Waqf Policies

The experiences of waqf management in the Middle East, Southeast Asia, and Turkey offer valuable insights for shaping

India's waqf policies. India, with its significant Muslim population and diverse cultural context, faces unique challenges and opportunities in waqf administration.

**Current State of Waqf in India:** India has a long history of waqf institutions, with a legal framework that has evolved over time:

1. Legal Framework: The primary legislation governing waqfs in India is the Waqf Act of 1995, which was amended in 2013 to address various issues in waqf management.

2. Administrative Structure: Each state has its own Waqf Board, with a Central Waqf Council at the national level providing oversight and coordination.

3. Challenges: Indian waqfs face numerous challenges, including encroachment of waqf properties, lack of proper surveys, and inefficient management.

**Proposed Reforms and Controversies:** The Indian government has proposed several reforms to the waqf system, as outlined in the Waqf (Amendment) Bill 2024. However, these proposals have sparked controversy and debate:

1. Centralization: The bill proposes to empower district collectors to determine the status of waqf properties, which some see as an attempt to centralize control.

2. Representation: The bill suggests including non-Muslim members in waqf boards, which has been criticized as diluting the Muslim character of waqf institutions.

3. Legal Status: There are proposals to repeal older waqf laws and create a more "Indianized" system, which has raised concerns about the preservation of waqf's Islamic character.

**Lessons from International Experiences:** Drawing from the experiences of other countries, India could consider the following approaches in shaping its waqf policies:

1. Balancing Tradition and Modernization: Like Turkey, India could seek ways to modernize waqf management while respecting its religious and cultural significance. This could involve updating legal frameworks to allow for more flexible and productive use of waqf assets while maintaining their core charitable purposes.

2. Professionalization: Following the example of Southeast Asian countries like Malaysia and Singapore, India could focus on professionalizing waqf management. This could include:

- Establishing specialized education and training programs for waqf administrators.
- Implementing modern financial management and auditing practices.
- Encouraging research and innovation in waqf development.

3. Transparency and Accountability: Adopting transparent reporting mechanisms and regular audits, as seen in Singapore's waqf system, could help build trust and efficiency in India's waqf administration.

4. Diversification of Waqf Forms: India could explore innovative waqf instruments, such as cash waqfs and corporate waqfs, which have been successfully implemented in countries like Malaysia.

5. Community Involvement: Drawing from the Middle Eastern experience, India could seek ways to increase beneficiary participation in waqf management, potentially through advisory boards or community consultations.

6. Asset Enhancement: Following Singapore's example, India could implement strategies to enhance the value and productivity of waqf properties, ensuring their long-term sustainability and increased benefit to the community.

7. Collaboration and Knowledge Sharing: India could benefit

from establishing networks for knowledge sharing and collaboration with other countries experienced in waqf management, particularly in the Islamic world.

**Addressing Concerns and Controversies**: In implementing reforms, it's crucial for India to address the concerns raised by various stakeholders:

1. Preserving Religious Character: Any reforms should balance modernization with respect for the Islamic character of waqf institutions, addressing concerns about dilution of Muslim representation in waqf management.

2. Protecting Waqf Assets: Strengthening legal protections against encroachment and unauthorized sale of waqf properties should be a priority.

3. Ensuring Autonomy: While improving oversight, reforms should avoid excessive centralization that could undermine the autonomy of waqf institutions.

4. Inclusive Approach: Reforms should be developed through inclusive consultations with Muslim religious leaders, legal experts, and community representatives to ensure broad acceptance and support.

**References:**

1. https://www.tamimi.com/law-update-articles/the-new-waqf-islamic-trust-law-in-the-emirate-of-sharjah/

2. https://law.yale.edu/sites/default/files/documents/pdf/Intellectual_Life/LTW-Kuran.pdf

3. https://www.elgaronline.com/abstract/book/9781803929804/book-part-9781803929804-12.xml

4. https://epiiecons.usim.edu.my/index.php/eproceeding/article/view/99

5. https://islamicmarkets.com/education/survival-restoration-of-waqfs-in-turkey

6.      http://journalarticle.ukm.my/23117/1/IJIT_24_3.pdf
7.      https://www.cenfa.org/economic-and-financial-implications-of-the-waqf-amendment-bill-2024-a-muslim-perspective/
8.      https://www.business-standard.com/india-news/decoded-how-is-a-waqf-created-and-what-are-the-powers-of-waqf-board-124080500469_1.html
9.      https://en.wikipedia.org/wiki/Waqf
10.     https://journals.iium.edu.my/intdiscourse/index.php/id/article/download/1264/832
11.     https://www.hindustantimes.com/opinion/political-implications-of-the-proposed-waqf-law-101733063123186.html
12.     https://www.theindiaforum.in/law/wakf-reforms-or-bid-control-waqf-properties

## *Chapter 24: Ethical Considerations in Waqf Administration*

The institution of waqf has played a critical role in the development of Muslim civilization, with contributions that extend beyond typical charitable functions (Alomair, 2018). As waqf institutions undergo revival and reform, there is an increasing need to apply robust governance systems and ethical practices to improve their performance, transparency, and accountability. This chapter examines the key ethical considerations in waqf administration, focusing on principles of honesty and integrity, addressing corruption, building trust, and ensuring just distribution.

**Principles of Honesty and Integrity:** Honesty and integrity form the bedrock of ethical waqf administration. The JAWHAR Code of Ethics, developed by the Department of Awqaf, Zakat and Hajj in Malaysia, provides a useful framework based on the principles of "HIJRAH":

H - Hemah dan beradab (Respectful and courteous)

I - Ikhlas (Sincerity)

J - Jujur (Honesty)

R - Rajin (Diligence)

A - Amanah (Trustworthiness)

H - Hebat (Excellence)

This code emphasizes values such as integrity, transparency, professionalism, courtesy, punctuality, and knowledge that should be upheld by waqf administrators (Kamri, 2010). By adhering to these principles, waqf institutions can create a professional culture and restore the glory attained in the past.

Honesty in waqf administration extends to accurate record-keeping, transparent reporting, and truthful communication with stakeholders. Waqf managers must provide clear and comprehensive information about the assets under their care, the revenues generated, and how funds are utilized. This transparency builds credibility and allows beneficiaries and donors to trust that their contributions are being used as intended.

Integrity in decision-making is equally crucial. Waqf administrators must make choices that align with the waqif's (founder's) intentions and benefit the intended recipients, rather than serving personal interests or those of influential parties. This may involve resisting pressure from powerful individuals or groups seeking to exploit waqf resources for their own gain.

**Addressing Corruption in Waqf Management:** Corruption poses a significant threat to the ethical administration of waqf properties. Various forms of corruption have been identified in waqf management, including:

1. Embezzlement of funds

2. Illegal occupation or encroachment of waqf lands

3. Undervaluation of waqf properties for personal gain

4. Nepotism in appointing waqf managers or beneficiaries

5. Misuse of waqf assets for non-intended purposes

The scale of corruption in waqf administration is alarming. In India, for example, it has been reported that almost 70% of waqf property has been encroached upon, with the remaining properties often subject to blatant corruption (Deccan Herald, 2009). Land is frequently disposed of to builders, markets, hotels, malls, or industries at shockingly low rents, depriving the intended beneficiaries of valuable resources.To address these issues, several measures can be implemented:

1. Strengthening legal frameworks: Governments should enact and enforce robust laws specifically tailored to protect waqf properties and punish corrupt practices.

2. Improving governance structures: Establishing clear lines of authority, responsibility, and accountability within waqf institutions can help prevent and detect corrupt activities.

3. Implementing rigorous auditing processes: Regular, independent audits can uncover financial irregularities and ensure compliance with ethical standards.

4. Enhancing transparency: Making waqf records, financial statements, and decision-making processes publicly accessible can deter corrupt practices and facilitate public scrutiny.

5. Professionalizing waqf management: Appointing qualified, competent individuals to manage waqf properties can reduce the likelihood of corruption and improve overall administration.

6. Leveraging technology: Implementing digital systems for record-keeping, asset management, and financial transactions can increase efficiency and reduce opportunities for corruption.

7. Encouraging whistleblowing: Establishing protected channels for reporting suspected corruption can help uncover and address unethical practices.

By implementing these measures, waqf institutions can work towards eliminating corruption and ensuring that resources are used as intended by the waqif for the benefit of the designated beneficiaries.

## Building Trust Among Beneficiaries

Trust is a critical component in the successful administration of waqf properties. When beneficiaries and the wider community trust waqf institutions, they are more likely to support and contribute to these endowments, ensuring their long-term sustainability and impact.

Research has shown that good governance and transparent reporting practices play a crucial role in building trust in waqf management (Alomair, 2018). Key factors that contribute to trust-building include:

1. Accountability: Waqf administrators must be accountable for their actions and decisions. This involves regular reporting on the status of waqf properties, financial performance, and the impact of waqf-funded programs.

2. Transparency: Open communication about waqf operations, decision-making processes, and challenges faced can help beneficiaries understand and appreciate the work of waqf institutions.

3. Competence: Demonstrating professional management and effective utilization of waqf resources builds confidence in the institution's ability to fulfill its mandate.

4. Consistency: Adhering consistently to ethical principles and stated objectives reinforces trust over time.

5. Responsiveness: Being attentive and responsive to the needs and concerns of beneficiaries' shows that the waqf institution values their input and is committed to serving them effectively.

6. Stakeholder engagement: Actively involving beneficiaries and other stakeholders in decision-making processes can foster a sense of ownership and trust in the waqf institution.

To operationalize these trust-building factors, waqf institutions can:

- Publish regular, detailed reports on waqf activities, financial performance, and impact
- Establish clear communication channels for beneficiaries to provide feedback and raise concerns
- Conduct regular stakeholder consultations to

> understand evolving needs and expectations
> - Implement a robust performance measurement system to demonstrate the effectiveness of waqf programs
> - Provide training and development opportunities for waqf administrators to enhance their competence and professionalism

By focusing on these trust-building measures, waqf institutions can create a virtuous cycle where increased trust leads to greater support, enabling more effective fulfillment of the waqf's objectives.

## Ensuring Justice in Waqf Distribution

Justice in waqf distribution is a fundamental ethical consideration that aligns with the Islamic principles of fairness and equity. Waqf administrators must ensure that the benefits of waqf properties are distributed in accordance with the waqif's intentions and in a manner that promotes social justice. Several aspects of just distribution in waqf administration should be considered:

1. Adherence to the waqif's stipulations: The primary ethical obligation of waqf administrators is to respect and implement the conditions set by the waqif, as long as they do not contradict Shariah law (Wedlake Bell, n.d.). This may include specific instructions on beneficiary selection, distribution methods, or prioritization of needs.

2. Equitable treatment of beneficiaries: In cases where the waqif has not specified detailed conditions, beneficiaries should generally be treated equally. For example, in a family waqf (Waqf Ahli), male and female descendants should receive equal benefits unless otherwise stipulated (Wedlake Bell, n.d.).

3. Prioritization based on need: When distributing waqf benefits, administrators should consider the relative needs of

potential beneficiaries, ensuring that those in greatest need receive appropriate support.

4. Transparency in selection criteria: The criteria and processes for selecting beneficiaries should be clear, consistent, and publicly available to prevent accusations of favoritism or discrimination.

5. Balancing short-term and long-term objectives: Waqf administrators must strike a balance between meeting immediate needs and preserving the waqf's assets for future generations.

6. Addressing changing circumstances: As societal needs evolve, waqf administrators may need to adapt distribution strategies while remaining true to the waqif's original intentions.

7. Avoiding conflicts of interest: Administrators should have mechanisms in place to prevent personal interests from influencing distribution decisions.

To implement these principles of just distribution, waqf institutions can:

- Develop clear, written policies and procedures for beneficiary selection and distribution
- Establish independent committees to oversee distribution decisions
- Regularly review and update distribution strategies to ensure they remain relevant and effective
- Implement monitoring and evaluation systems to assess the impact of waqf distributions on beneficiaries
- Provide channels for beneficiaries to appeal decisions or raise concerns about distribution practices

By focusing on justice in distribution, waqf institutions can fulfill their ethical obligations, maximize the impact of their resources, and contribute to broader social equity.

In conclusion, ethical considerations play a crucial role in the effective administration of waqf properties. By upholding principles of honesty and integrity, addressing corruption, building trust among beneficiaries, and ensuring just distribution, waqf institutions can maximize their positive impact on society and fulfill their sacred mandate. As the institution of waqf continues to evolve and adapt to modern challenges, maintaining a strong ethical foundation will be essential for its continued relevance and success in serving the needs of Muslim communities and beyond.

**References:**


1. Alomair, M. (2018). Governance and accountability in corporate waqf institutions in Saudi Arabia (Doctoral dissertation). Royal Holloway, University of London.
2. Deccan Herald. (2009, October 18). In the name of Allah: Waqf corruption in India. Retrieved from https://www.deccanherald.com/content/31093/in-name-allah-waqf-corruption.html
3. Kamri, N. A. (2010). The roles of ethics in waqf management: Case of JAWHAR. Shariah Journal, 18(3), 659-680.
4. Wedlake Bell. (n.d.). Trusts in Islamic Law. Retrieved from https://wedlakebell.com/trusts-islamic-law/

## Chapter 25: Public Awareness and Waqf

The institution of waqf has played a crucial role in Islamic societies for centuries, serving as a powerful instrument for social and economic development. However, in recent times, there has been a growing need to revitalize and promote awareness about waqf among Muslim communities worldwide. This chapter explores the importance of educating Muslims about waqf, the role of media in promoting waqf awareness, community engagement in protecting waqf properties, and outreach programs for rural areas.

### Importance of Educating Muslims about Waqf

Waqf, an Islamic endowment system, has been a cornerstone of Muslim philanthropy and social welfare for centuries. However, in many contemporary Muslim societies, there is a lack of understanding and awareness about the significance and potential of waqf. Educating Muslims about waqf is crucial for several reasons:

### Preserving Islamic Heritage

Waqf is deeply rooted in Islamic tradition, tracing back to the time of Prophet Muhammad (peace be upon him). The Prophet himself established the first waqf in Islamic history, and his companions followed suit. For instance, Umar bin Khattab donated a piece of land in Khaibar as waqf. By educating Muslims about waqf, we ensure the preservation of this important aspect of Islamic heritage and its continued relevance in modern times.

### Promoting Sustainable Development

Waqf has the potential to be a powerful tool for sustainable development in Muslim communities. It can provide a continuous source of funding for various social, educational, and economic initiatives. For example, throughout Islamic history, waqf has been used to support educational institutions, ensuring the development and dissemination of knowledge. By understanding the potential of waqf, Muslims can contribute to long-term community development projects that have lasting impact.

## Encouraging Philanthropy

Education about waqf can inspire more Muslims to engage in philanthropic activities. When people understand the spiritual rewards and social benefits associated with waqf, they are more likely to contribute. This increased participation can lead to a significant expansion of resources available for community welfare and development.

## Addressing Contemporary Challenges

Many Muslim communities face challenges in areas such as education, healthcare, and poverty alleviation. By educating Muslims about how waqf can be utilized to address these issues, communities can mobilize resources more effectively. For instance, waqf can be used to establish and maintain educational institutions, providing access to quality education for underprivileged children.

## Enhancing Financial Literacy

Education about waqf also contributes to improving financial literacy among Muslims. It introduces concepts of long-term investment, asset management, and sustainable financial planning for charitable purposes. This knowledge can have positive spillover effects on personal financial management as well.

**Role of Media in Promoting Waqf Awareness:** In the digital age, media plays a crucial role in shaping public opinion and disseminating information. When it comes to promoting waqf awareness, various forms of media can be leveraged effectively:

## Social Media Platforms

Social media has emerged as a powerful tool for raising awareness about waqf. Platforms like Facebook, Instagram, and YouTube offer opportunities to reach a wide audience, especially younger generations. Research has shown that social media can have a significant influence on waqf funding. A study on BPW Ar Risalah found that social media activity contributed to an increase in the number of waqifs (donors) participating in waqf programs.

## Digital Content Creation

Creating engaging and informative digital content about waqf can help increase public understanding. This can include educational videos, infographics, and articles distributed across various online platforms. The Indonesian Waqf Board, for example, provides waqf literacy content in the form of digital books, articles, graphics, and videos on their website and social media channels.

## Mobile Applications

Developing mobile applications dedicated to waqf can make information and participation more accessible. These apps can provide educational content, facilitate donations, and offer real-time updates on waqf projects. The ease of use and accessibility of mobile apps can encourage more people to engage with waqf initiatives.

## Traditional Media

While digital media is increasingly important, traditional media outlets such as television, radio, and print newspapers still play a significant role in reaching certain demographics. Collaborating with these media outlets to produce programs or articles about waqf can help reach a broader audience.

## Influencer Partnerships

Partnering with social media influencers, religious leaders, and community figures can amplify the message about waqf. These individuals can use their platforms to educate their followers about the importance and benefits of waqf.

## Interactive Platforms

Creating interactive online platforms where people can learn about waqf, ask questions, and engage in discussions can foster a deeper understanding of the concept. This can include webinars, online workshops, and Q&A sessions with waqf experts.

## Community Engagement in Protecting Waqf Properties

Community involvement is crucial for the protection and proper management of waqf properties. Engaging the community not only helps in safeguarding these assets but also fosters a sense of ownership and responsibility among community members. Here are some key aspects of community engagement in protecting waqf properties:

## Awareness Campaigns

Organizing awareness campaigns at the community level is essential for educating people about the importance of waqf properties and their role in protecting them. These campaigns can include workshops, seminars, and community meetings where experts can share information about waqf and its significance.

## Community Watch Groups

Forming community watch groups can be an effective way to monitor and protect waqf properties. These groups can consist of local volunteers who keep an eye on waqf assets and report any suspicious activities or encroachments. This grassroots approach ensures constant vigilance and quick response to potential threats.

## Collaboration with Local Authorities

Encouraging collaboration between community members and local authorities is crucial for effective protection of waqf properties. This can involve regular meetings with local law enforcement, municipal bodies, and waqf boards to address concerns and develop strategies for property protection.

## Legal Awareness and Support

Providing legal awareness to community members about waqf laws and regulations empowers them to take appropriate action when needed. Additionally, establishing a network of legal experts who can offer pro bono services for waqf-related issues can be invaluable in protecting these properties.

## Technology-Enabled Monitoring

Leveraging technology for community-based monitoring of waqf properties can enhance protection efforts. This can include using mobile apps for reporting issues, creating digital databases of waqf properties, and using GIS mapping for better management and monitoring.

## Youth Engagement

Involving young people in waqf protection initiatives is crucial for long-term sustainability. This can be done through educational programs in schools and colleges, youth-led community service projects focused on waqf properties, and internship opportunities with waqf management organizations.

## Interfaith Cooperation

In diverse communities, fostering interfaith cooperation for the protection of waqf properties can promote social harmony and mutual respect. This can involve joint initiatives between different religious communities to protect and preserve religious and cultural heritage sites.

## Transparency and Accountability

Promoting transparency in the management of waqf properties builds trust within the community. Regular public reporting on the status and use of waqf assets encourages community members to stay involved and vigilant.

**Outreach Programs for Rural Areas:** Extending waqf awareness and education to rural areas is crucial for ensuring the comprehensive development and utilization of waqf resources. Rural communities often have limited access to information and resources, making targeted outreach programs essential. Here are some strategies for effective waqf outreach in rural areas:

## Mobile Education Units

Implementing mobile education units that can travel to remote rural areas can be an effective way to spread awareness about waqf. These units can be equipped with educational materials, audiovisual aids, and trained personnel to conduct workshops and seminars in villages and small towns.

## Collaboration with Local Institutions

Partnering with local institutions such as mosques, madrasas, and community centers can provide established platforms for waqf education. These institutions often have the trust of the local community and can facilitate the dissemination of information effectively.

## Tailored Educational Materials

Developing educational materials that are culturally appropriate and easily understandable for rural populations is crucial. This may include using local languages, visual aids, and relatable examples that resonate with rural life experiences.

## Training Local Advocates

Identifying and training local community members as waqf

advocates can create a sustainable model for ongoing education and awareness. These local advocates can serve as long-term resources for their communities, providing information and guidance on waqf-related matters.

## Leveraging Traditional Communication Channels

In rural areas where digital penetration may be limited, utilizing traditional communication channels such as community radio, local newspapers, and town hall meetings can be effective in reaching a wider audience.

## Integrating Waqf Education with Rural Development Programs

Incorporating waqf education into existing rural development programs can provide a holistic approach to community empowerment. This can include integrating waqf concepts into agricultural extension services, microfinance initiatives, and rural health programs.

## Demonstrating Practical Applications

Showcasing successful waqf projects that have benefited rural communities can inspire and motivate others to participate. This can include organizing field visits to waqf-funded schools, healthcare facilities, or agricultural projects in rural areas.

## Addressing Rural-Specific Needs

Tailoring waqf education to address specific needs and challenges faced by rural communities can increase relevance and engagement. This might include focusing on how waqf can support agricultural development, rural infrastructure, or access to education and healthcare.

In conclusion, public awareness and education about waqf are crucial for revitalizing this important Islamic institution in contemporary times. By leveraging various media platforms, engaging communities in the protection of waqf properties, and implementing targeted outreach programs for rural areas, we can ensure that waqf continues to serve as a powerful tool for social and economic development in Muslim societies. The collective efforts of religious institutions, educational bodies, media organizations, and community leaders are essential in this endeavor to harness the full potential of waqf for the betterment of society.

**References:**


1.    IRMA International. (n.d.). Waqf Education for Economic Growth. Retrieved from https://www.irma-international.org/viewtitle/244767/?isxn=9781799812456

2.    Jurnal STEI Ar Risalah. (n.d.). The Influence of Social Media on Waqf Funding In BPW Ar Risalah. Retrieved from http://jurnal.steiarrisalah.ac.id/index.php/stei/article/download/67/24/465

3.    Atlantis Press. (n.d.). Waqf Literacy Strategy for Empowering Waqf Based on Digital Media Platforms. Retrieved from https://www.atlantis-press.com/article/126003679.pdf

4.    Radiance Weekly. (n.d.). Citizens' Participation in Protecting Waqf Properties. Retrieved from https://radianceweekly.net/citizens-participation-in-protecting-waqf-properties/

5.    India Tomorrow. (2024, February 22). Community vigilance, awareness key to protect Waqf assets. Retrieved from https://indiatomorrow.net/2024/02/22/community-vigilance-awareness-key-to-protect-waqf-assets-call-from-bangalore-workshop/

6.    AIP Publishing. (n.d.). The introduction of waqf to empower the economic potential of rural communities. Retrieved from https://pubs.aip.org/aip/acp/article/2722/1/060003/2904783/The-introduction-of-waqf-to-empower-the-economic

7.	International British Waqf. (2024, October 15). Education Waqf. Retrieved from https://ibwaqf.org.uk/donate/projects/education-waqf

## *Chapter 26: The Role of*
## *Technology in Waqf Protection*

Technology has emerged as a powerful tool in protecting and managing waqf properties, offering innovative solutions to longstanding challenges faced by waqf institutions. This chapter explores four key technological applications that are revolutionizing waqf protection: satellite imaging for property surveys, blockchain for transparent record-keeping, GIS mapping of waqf properties, and mobile apps for reporting encroachments.

**Satellite Imaging for Waqf Property Surveys**

Satellite imaging technology has become an invaluable asset in surveying and monitoring waqf properties, particularly in addressing the persistent issue of encroachment. This advanced technology allows waqf administrators to conduct comprehensive surveys of large areas efficiently and accurately, providing a bird's-eye view of waqf lands and their surroundings.

One of the primary advantages of satellite imaging is its ability to detect and monitor changes in land use over time. By comparing historical satellite images with current ones, waqf managers can identify unauthorized constructions, encroachments, or alterations to waqf properties. This capability is particularly crucial for waqf lands located in remote or inaccessible areas, where regular physical inspections may be challenging or costly.

The implementation of satellite imaging in waqf management has shown promising results. For instance, in India, the Waqf Management System has incorporated satellite imagery analysis to detect encroachments on waqf properties. The system overlays GPS coordinates of waqf properties on historical satellite images, allowing administrators to pinpoint when and where encroachments occurred. This approach has proven effective in identifying and addressing unauthorized use of waqf lands.

Moreover, satellite imaging can assist in the initial surveying and documentation of waqf properties. Many waqf institutions face challenges in maintaining accurate records of their land holdings, especially for properties that have been in existence for centuries. Satellite imagery can provide up-to-date visual documentation of these properties, helping to establish clear boundaries and prevent future disputes.

The integration of satellite imaging with other technologies, such as Geographic Information Systems (GIS), further enhances its utility. This combination allows for the creation of detailed, layered maps that include not only the physical boundaries of waqf properties but also relevant information such as land use classification, nearby infrastructure, and demographic data. Such comprehensive mapping aids in strategic planning and development of waqf lands.

However, it's important to note that while satellite imaging is a powerful tool, it should be used in conjunction with ground-level verification. Satellite images may not capture all details or recent changes, and interpretation of these images requires expertise. Therefore, a balanced approach combining satellite technology with traditional surveying methods is often most effective.

## Blockchain for Transparent Record-Keeping

Blockchain technology has emerged as a revolutionary solution for enhancing transparency and security in waqf management. This decentralized digital ledger system offers immutable record-keeping capabilities that can address many of the challenges faced by waqf institutions in maintaining accurate and tamper-proof records.

The application of blockchain in waqf management can significantly improve transparency and trust in the system. Every transaction or change in waqf property status can be recorded on the blockchain, creating an unalterable audit trail. This level of transparency can help prevent fraud, mismanagement, and unauthorized alterations to waqf records, which have been persistent issues in traditional waqf administration.

One of the key advantages of blockchain is its ability to create smart contracts. These self-executing contracts with the terms of the agreement directly written into code can automate many aspects of waqf management. For instance, smart contracts can be programmed to automatically distribute waqf benefits to designated beneficiaries, ensuring timely and accurate disbursement of funds.

Blockchain also offers a solution to the challenge of fragmented record-keeping systems across different waqf institutions. By creating a unified, decentralized database, blockchain can facilitate better coordination and information sharing among various stakeholders involved in waqf management. This can lead to more efficient administration and reduce the likelihood of conflicting claims or duplicate records.

Several countries have begun exploring the potential of blockchain in waqf management. For example, in Singapore, a financial technology company has developed a blockchain-based crowdfunding platform for waqf projects. This platform uses smart contracts to manage fundraising and project implementation, enhancing transparency and efficiency in the process.

In Malaysia, there is growing interest in implementing blockchain for zakat management, which could potentially be extended to waqf administration. The technology's ability to provide security, transparency, and traceability for each transaction makes it an attractive option for managing Islamic social finance instruments.

However, the implementation of blockchain in waqf management is not without challenges. It requires significant technological infrastructure and expertise, which may be lacking in many traditional waqf institutions. Additionally, there may be regulatory hurdles to overcome, as blockchain technology often operates in a legal grey area in many jurisdictions.

Despite these challenges, the potential benefits of blockchain in enhancing transparency, security, and efficiency in waqf management are substantial. As the technology matures and becomes more widely adopted, it is likely to play an increasingly important role in modernizing waqf administration and protecting waqf assets.

## GIS Mapping of Waqf Properties

Geographic Information System (GIS) mapping has emerged as a crucial tool in the management and protection of waqf properties. This technology combines geographical features with tabular data to map, analyze, and assess real-world problems. In the context of waqf management, GIS offers a powerful means of visualizing, managing, and analyzing spatial data related to waqf properties.

The application of GIS in waqf management provides numerous benefits. Firstly, it allows for the creation of accurate, up-to-date digital maps of waqf properties. These maps can include detailed information about each property, such as its boundaries, size, current use, and legal status. This comprehensive mapping helps in preventing encroachments and resolving boundary disputes, which are common issues in waqf management.

GIS mapping also facilitates better decision-making in waqf property development and utilization. By overlaying various data layers - such as land use patterns, demographic information, and infrastructure details - on waqf property maps, administrators can make informed decisions about how best to develop or utilize these properties for maximum benefit. This data-driven approach can lead to more effective use of waqf assets and potentially increase their revenue-generating potential.

In India, the implementation of GIS mapping for waqf properties has shown significant promise. The Waqf Assets Management System of India (WAMSI) has integrated GIS mapping based on GPS coordinates of waqf properties. This system allows for the precise demarcation of waqf lands and helps in detecting encroachments by comparing current property boundaries with historical data.

The effectiveness of GIS in waqf management is evident from its implementation in various states. For instance, in Selangor, Malaysia, a study found that GIS mapping of waqf lands provided accurate cadastral maps, defining legal repositioning of ex-land ownership, status, and location. This enhanced systematic planning and management of waqf lands in the state.

Moreover, GIS mapping can be particularly useful in managing large portfolios of waqf properties. In Selangor alone, there were 832 recorded lots of waqf land as of 2021. GIS allows for efficient management of such large numbers of properties, providing a clear overview of their distribution, usage, and potential.

The integration of GIS with other technologies further enhances its utility. For example, combining GIS with remote sensing technologies allows for regular monitoring of waqf properties. Satellite or drone imagery can be overlaid on GIS maps to detect any changes or encroachments on waqf lands.

However, the successful implementation of GIS in waqf management requires overcoming certain challenges. These include the need for accurate base data, which may be lacking in many areas, and the requirement for specialized skills in GIS technology. Additionally, there may be initial resistance to adopting new technologies in traditional waqf institutions.

Despite these challenges, the role of GIS in waqf protection is increasingly recognized as essential. Its ability to provide accurate, visual representations of waqf properties, combined with powerful analytical capabilities, makes it an indispensable tool for modern waqf management.

**Mobile Apps for Reporting Encroachments**

The proliferation of smartphones and mobile technology has opened up new avenues for protecting waqf properties, particularly through the development of mobile applications designed for reporting encroachments. These apps leverage the widespread availability of mobile devices to create a network of vigilant citizens who can assist in monitoring and protecting waqf lands.

Mobile apps for reporting encroachments typically allow users to quickly and easily report any suspected unauthorized use or occupation of waqf properties. These apps often include features such as GPS location tagging, the ability to upload photos or videos of the encroachment, and a simple interface for describing the nature of the violation.

The advantages of using mobile apps for this purpose are numerous. Firstly, they enable real-time reporting of encroachments, allowing waqf administrators to respond quickly to potential threats to waqf properties. This immediacy can be crucial in preventing long-term occupation or damage to waqf lands.

Secondly, these apps can significantly expand the monitoring capacity of waqf institutions. Instead of relying solely on limited staff for property inspections, waqf boards can harness the power of community participation. This crowdsourcing approach can be particularly effective in monitoring large or geographically dispersed waqf properties.

While specific examples of mobile apps for reporting waqf encroachments are not widely documented in the literature, similar applications have been successfully used in other areas of land management and conservation. The principles and technologies used in these apps can be readily adapted for waqf protection.

For instance, in India, the Waqf Assets Management System of India (WAMSI) has developed an online portal that allows public access to information about waqf properties. While not specifically a mobile app, this system demonstrates the potential for leveraging technology to increase transparency and public participation in waqf protection.

The development of such mobile apps, however, comes with its own set of challenges. These include ensuring the accuracy of reported information, protecting the privacy of users, and managing the potentially large volume of reports. Additionally, there needs to be a robust system in place to verify and act upon the reports received through these apps.

Despite these challenges, the potential of mobile apps in protecting waqf properties is significant. They offer a cost-effective, scalable solution for monitoring waqf lands and can play a crucial role in early detection and prevention of encroachments.

The role of technology in waqf protection is increasingly crucial in the face of modern challenges to waqf management. Satellite imaging provides a powerful tool for surveying and monitoring large areas of waqf land, enabling early detection of encroachments and unauthorized changes. Blockchain technology offers a revolutionary approach to transparent and secures record-keeping, addressing longstanding issues of trust and accountability in waqf administration. GIS mapping provides a comprehensive visual and analytical tool for managing waqf properties, enhancing decision-making and strategic planning. Finally, mobile apps for reporting encroachments leverage community participation to create a more robust monitoring system for waqf lands.

While the implementation of these technologies faces challenges, including the need for infrastructure development, specialized skills, and potential regulatory hurdles, their potential benefits are substantial. As waqf institutions continue to modernize and adapt to contemporary challenges, the integration of these technological solutions will be crucial in ensuring the protection and effective management of waqf properties for future generations.

The successful implementation of these technologies requires a concerted effort from various stakeholders, including waqf administrators, technology experts, policymakers, and the community at large. By embracing these technological advancements, waqf institutions can enhance their capacity to fulfill their noble mission of serving society and preserving the legacy of Islamic philanthropy.

**References**


1. Abd Razak, A., Abu Bakar, M. F., & Abdullah, M. (2020). Blockchain for Islamic social finance. International Journal of Management and Applied Research, 7(4), 291-303.
2. AlTaei, F., Barghuthi, N. A., & Said, H. (2018). Blockchain approach for smart city. In 2018 International Conference on Smart Communications and Networking (SmartNets) (pp. 1-6). IEEE.
3. Alharthi, M. (2021). Blockchain technology in Islamic finance: A systematic literature review. Journal of Islamic Marketing, 12(8), 1503-1520.

4.      Bouakkaz, M. (2022). Blockchain technology and its applications in Islamic finance. International Journal of Islamic Economics and Finance Studies, 8(1), 55-76.

5.      Government of India. (2023). Property of Waqf Board. Press Information Bureau. https://pib.gov.in/PressReleaseIframePage.aspx?PRID=1895837

6.      Kasmon, B., Ibrahim, S.S., Daud, D., Raja Hisham, R.R.I. and Ratnasari, R.T. (2024). Future behavior in waqf digitalization: integrating UTAUT and DIT. Journal of Islamic Marketing, ahead-of-print. https://doi.org/10.1108/JIMA-03-2024-0111

7.      Nik Mohd Saiful W Mohd Sidik, & Zaid Ahmad. (2021). Application of GIS (Geographical Information System) in The Management of Waqf Lands in Selangor. International Journal of Academic Research in Business and Social Sciences, 11(11), 1642-1651.

8.      Widiastuti, T., Rusydiana, A. S., Robani, A., Insani, T. D., & Muryani. (2020). Obstacles and strategies in implementing blockchain technology in waqf management: A bibliometric analysis. Library Philosophy and Practice, 1-19.

9.      WAMSI. (n.d.). National WAMSI Project. https://wakf.gov.in/homepage/about_project.php

---

## Chapter 27: Waqf and Environmental Sustainability

In recent years, the intersection of Islamic finance and environmental sustainability has gained significant attention, with waqf (Islamic endowment) emerging as a powerful tool for addressing ecological challenges. This chapter explores the multifaceted relationship between waqf and environmental sustainability, examining how this centuries-old Islamic institution can be leveraged to promote eco-friendly initiatives, preserve natural resources, and integrate environmental considerations into waqf property management.

**Eco-Friendly Projects on Waqf Lands:** Waqf lands offer a unique opportunity for implementing eco-friendly projects that align with both Islamic principles and environmental conservation goals. The perpetual nature of waqf makes it an ideal vehicle for long-term environmental initiatives.

## Reforestation and Afforestation

One of the most prominent eco-friendly projects on waqf lands is reforestation and afforestation. These initiatives not only contribute to carbon sequestration but also help restore ecosystems and protect biodiversity. In Indonesia, for example, the concept of "Waqf Forest" has gained traction since 2012, particularly in response to the conversion of Aceh forest lands. These waqf forests serve multiple purposes:

1. Improving ecosystems and maintaining air and water quality

2. Reducing global warming

3. Maintaining soil fertility

4. Providing sources for food and medicine

5. Preventing natural disasters

## Renewable Energy Projects

Waqf lands can also be utilized for renewable energy projects, such as solar farms or wind turbines. These initiatives align with the Islamic principle of stewardship over the earth while contributing to the transition towards clean energy. For instance, the Indonesian Waqf Board has been exploring the potential of using waqf assets to develop renewable energy infrastructure.

## Sustainable Agriculture

Implementing sustainable agricultural practices on waqf lands can promote food security while preserving the environment. In Turkey, agricultural waqf projects support sustainable farming practices, using organic techniques that protect the environment while contributing to food security.

## Water Conservation

Waqf properties can be dedicated to water conservation projects, such as rainwater harvesting systems or the restoration of water bodies. These initiatives are particularly crucial in regions facing water scarcity.

**Role of Waqf in Promoting Green Initiatives:** Waqf plays significant role in promoting green initiatives by providing a sustainable funding mechanism and aligning environmental conservation with Islamic principles.

## Green Waqf Framework

The concept of "Green Waqf" has emerged as a contemporary adaptation of the traditional waqf model, focusing specifically on environmental sustainability. The Green Waqf Framework, developed by the Indonesia Waqf Board in collaboration with the United Nations Development Programme (UNDP), provides a comprehensive guideline for implementing environmentally-focused waqf projects.The framework outlines a four-stage model for Green Waqf initiatives:

1. Planning and design

2. Implementation

3. Monitoring and evaluation

4. Scaling up and replication

This structured approach ensures that Green Waqf projects are well-conceived, effectively implemented, and capable of generating lasting environmental impact.

**Funding Mechanism for Environmental Projects**

Green Waqf serves as an innovative funding mechanism for environmental projects, addressing the significant financing gap often faced by developing countries in climate action. By establishing endowments specifically aimed at funding climate-related projects, Green Waqf provides a sustainable, long-term financing solution for environmental initiatives.

The perpetual nature of waqf makes it particularly suitable for environmental projects that require consistent, long-term funding. This characteristic sets waqf apart from other forms of Islamic charity, such as sadaqah or zakat, which are typically one-time or annual donations.

**Awareness and Education**

Waqf institutions can play a crucial role in raising awareness about environmental issues and promoting eco-friendly practices. By integrating environmental education into their programs, waqf organizations can foster a culture of environmental stewardship within communities.

**Community Engagement**

Many Green Waqf projects are designed to involve local communities through volunteer opportunities or educational programs. This approach not only helps raise awareness about environmental issues but also fosters a sense of ownership and responsibility among community members.

**Preservation of Natural Resources through Waqf:** Waqf can be instrumental in preserving natural resources, aligning with the Islamic principle of environmental stewardship.

## Land Conservation

Dedicating land as waqf for conservation purposes ensures its long-term protection from development or exploitation. This approach can be particularly effective in preserving critical habitats, biodiversity hotspots, or ecologically sensitive areas.

## Water Resource Management

Waqf can be used to protect and manage water resources. Historical examples, such as the waqf-funded water systems in the city of Shiraz, demonstrate how waqf can be used to ensure sustainable water supply and management.

**Biodiversity Conservation:** Establishing waqf for the purpose of biodiversity conservation can help protect endangered species and their habitats. This aligns with the Islamic principle of stewardship over all of God's creation.

## Sustainable Resource Utilization

Waqf properties can be managed in ways that promote sustainable resource utilization. For example, waqf forests can be managed to provide sustainable timber harvests while maintaining the overall health of the ecosystem.

**Integrating Waqf Properties into Environmental Policies:** The integration of waqf properties into broader environmental policies represents a significant opportunity to enhance the impact of both waqf and environmental conservation efforts.

## Policy Frameworks

Developing comprehensive policy frameworks that recognize and support the role of waqf in environmental conservation is crucial. These frameworks should address legal, financial, and governance aspects of environmental waqf.

## Collaboration with Environmental Agencies

Waqf institutions should collaborate closely with environmental agencies to ensure that waqf properties are managed in line with national and international environmental standards and goals.

## Alignment with Sustainable Development Goals (SDGs)

Green Waqf initiatives should be aligned with relevant Sustainable Development Goals, particularly SDG 13 (Climate Action), SDG 14 (Life Below Water), and SDG 15 (Life on Land). This alignment ensures that waqf efforts contribute to globally recognized sustainability targets.

## Innovative Financial Instruments

The integration of waqf into environmental policies can be facilitated through innovative financial instruments. For example, the development of "Green Sukuk" (Islamic bonds) linked to environmental waqf projects can attract a wider range of investors and increase funding for eco-friendly initiatives.

## Monitoring and Reporting Mechanisms

Establishing robust monitoring and reporting mechanisms for environmental waqf projects is essential. These mechanisms should track the environmental impact of waqf properties and ensure transparency in their management.

## Capacity Building

Investing in capacity building for waqf managers (nazirs) in environmental management and sustainable practices is crucial for the effective integration of waqf properties into environmental policies.

In conclusion, the integration of waqf and environmental sustainability represents a powerful synergy between Islamic principles and contemporary ecological needs. By leveraging the unique characteristics of waqf – its perpetuity, flexibility, and community-oriented nature – Muslim societies can make significant contributions to global environmental conservation efforts. The development of Green Waqf frameworks, the implementation of eco-friendly projects on waqf lands, and the integration of waqf into broader environmental policies all demonstrate the potential of this Islamic institution to address pressing environmental challenges.

As the world grapples with climate change, biodiversity loss, and resource depletion, the role of waqf in promoting environmental sustainability is likely to become increasingly important. By combining traditional Islamic values with modern environmental science and sustainable development practices, waqf can serve as a model for faith-based environmental stewardship, offering valuable lessons for both Muslim and non-Muslim societies alike.

The success of environmental waqf initiatives will depend on continued innovation, policy support, and community engagement. As more countries and institutions adopt and refine the concept of Green Waqf, its potential to drive meaningful environmental change will only grow. In this way, waqf can play a crucial role in ensuring a sustainable and environmentally sound future for generations to come, fulfilling its original purpose of perpetual benefit to society in a manner that addresses one of the most pressing challenges of our time.

**References:**

1.      Idllalène, S. (2024). The role of environmental Waqf in addressing climate change in the MENA region. In Climate

Change in the Middle East and North Africa. Routledge.

2.	Indonesia Waqf Board & United Nations Development Programme. (2024). Green Waqf Framework. UNDP Climate Promise.

3.	Siddiqui, A. (2024, October 21). Green Waqf for climate finance. Dawn.

4.	Ummah4Earth. (n.d.). Green Waqf: a sustainable approach to philanthropy.

5.	Lathif, A. A., Naim, A. M., Yusoff, R. M., Omar, N., & Rahman, A. A. (2024). A SWOT and Internal-External Factor Evaluation Analysis for Forest Waqf Implementation. International Journal of Environmental Impacts, 7(3), 1-12.

6.	Utama, A. S., Wahid, H., & Ahmad, S. (2024). Developing Green Waqf Model for Environmental Issues. Islamic Economics Methodology, 2(2).

## *Chapter 28: Global Contributions of Indian Waqf*

The institution of waqf in India has a rich history dating back to the early days of Islamic rule in the subcontinent. Over the centuries, it has evolved into a significant socio-economic force, not only within India but also on the global stage. This chapter explores the international recognition, collaborations, impacts, and future opportunities of Indian waqf institutions in the global context.

### Recognition of Indian Waqf Institutions Internationally

Indian waqf institutions have gained considerable recognition on the international stage, primarily due to their vast scale and potential for socio-economic development. With over 500,000 registered waqfs encompassing approximately 600,000 acres of land and an estimated book value of Rs. 60 billion, Indian waqf properties collectively represent one of the largest Islamic endowments in the world. This sheer magnitude has drawn attention from global Islamic organizations and scholars interested in studying and potentially replicating successful waqf management models.

The historical significance of Indian waqf institutions also contributes to their international recognition. The concept of waqf in India can be traced back to the Delhi Sultanate, with one of the earliest recorded instances being Sultan Muizuddin Sam Ghaor's dedication of two villages to the Jama Masjid of Multan. This long-standing tradition of Islamic philanthropy has positioned India as a key player in the global waqf landscape.

International recognition has also been bolstered by India's efforts to modernize and reform its waqf management systems. The Waqf Act of 1995, along with subsequent amendments, has created a more structured and transparent framework for waqf administration. These legal reforms have been studied by other countries seeking to improve their own waqf governance models.

Moreover, the potential of Indian waqf institutions to contribute to poverty alleviation and socio-economic development has garnered attention from international development agencies and Islamic financial institutions. The vast resources held by Indian waqfs, if effectively utilized, could play a crucial role in addressing social issues and promoting economic growth among Muslim communities.

**Collaboration with Global Islamic Organizations**

Indian waqf institutions have engaged in various collaborations with global Islamic organizations, fostering knowledge exchange and promoting best practices in waqf management. These partnerships have been instrumental in enhancing the capacity and effectiveness of Indian waqf boards and administrators.

One notable area of collaboration has been with international Islamic financial institutions. These partnerships have focused on developing innovative financial instruments and investment strategies to maximize the returns on waqf assets. By leveraging global expertise in Islamic finance, Indian waqf institutions have been exploring ways to enhance the productivity and sustainability of their endowments.

Collaborations have also extended to educational and research initiatives. Indian waqf scholars and administrators have participated in international conferences, seminars, and training programs organized by global Islamic organizations. These events have provided platforms for sharing experiences, discussing challenges, and exploring solutions to common issues faced by waqf institutions worldwide.

Furthermore, Indian waqf institutions have been actively involved in global efforts to standardize waqf practices and develop universal guidelines for waqf management. This participation has not only contributed to the global discourse on waqf but has also helped in aligning Indian waqf practices with international standards.

The Central Waqf Council of India, as the apex body overseeing waqf administration in the country, has played a pivotal role in fostering these international collaborations. By engaging with counterparts from other countries and participating in global forums, the Council has helped position Indian waqf institutions as key players in the international waqf community.

## Impact of Indian Waqf on the Islamic World

The impact of Indian waqf on the Islamic world has been multifaceted, encompassing historical, cultural, and socio-economic dimensions. Historically, the development of waqf institutions in India has been closely intertwined with the spread of Islam in the subcontinent. The establishment of mosques, madrasas, and charitable institutions through waqf endowments played a crucial role in the consolidation and propagation of Islamic culture and education in India.

One of the significant impacts of Indian waqf on the Islamic world has been in the realm of Islamic jurisprudence and legal frameworks governing waqf. The Mussalman Waqf Validating Act of 1913, which was advocated by Mohammad Ali Jinnah, was a landmark legislation that influenced waqf laws in other parts of the Islamic world. This Act, which validated family waqfs (waqf-alal-aulad) and provided them legal protection, set a precedent for similar legislations in other countries.

The scale and diversity of Indian waqf institutions have also contributed to the global discourse on the potential of waqf as a tool for socio-economic development. The experiences of Indian waqf boards in managing large portfolios of properties and navigating complex legal and administrative challenges have provided valuable insights for other Muslim-majority and

Muslim-minority countries grappling with similar issues.

Moreover, the Indian model of waqf administration, characterized by a mix of centralized oversight and decentralized management through state waqf boards, has been studied by other countries seeking to balance government regulation with community involvement in waqf management. The successes and challenges of this model have informed waqf governance reforms in various parts of the Islamic world.

The impact of Indian waqf extends to the realm of Islamic finance and economics as well. The efforts to revitalize and modernize waqf assets in India, including initiatives for better asset management and income generation, have contributed to the global conversation on leveraging waqf for economic empowerment and sustainable development.

**Future Opportunities for International Engagement**

As the global Islamic economy continues to grow and evolve, there are numerous opportunities for Indian waqf institutions to expand their international engagement and contribute to the development of the global waqf sector.

One key area of opportunity lies in the field of technology integration. Indian waqf institutions can leverage their experience in digitizing waqf records and implementing online management systems to collaborate with international partners on developing cutting-edge technologies for waqf administration. This could include blockchain-based solutions for transparent asset management, artificial intelligence for property valuation, and big data analytics for strategic decision-making.

Another promising avenue for international engagement is in the realm of Islamic social finance. Indian waqf institutions, with their vast asset base and experience in managing charitable endowments, are well-positioned to participate in global initiatives aimed at mobilizing Islamic philanthropic resources for sustainable development goals. Collaborations with international organizations such as the Islamic Development Bank and the World Bank could open up new channels for leveraging waqf assets to address global challenges like poverty, education, and healthcare.

There is also significant potential for Indian waqf institutions to engage in knowledge exchange programs with their counterparts in other countries. These programs could focus on sharing best practices in areas such as property development, investment strategies, and community engagement. By fostering a global network of waqf professionals, such initiatives could contribute to the overall advancement of waqf management practices worldwide.

Furthermore, Indian waqf institutions have the opportunity to play a more active role in global policy discussions on waqf. As countries around the world grapple with issues of waqf reform and regulation, the Indian experience – with its unique blend of historical legacy, legal framework, and administrative challenges – can provide valuable insights for policymakers and legislators.

The growing interest in Islamic heritage tourism presents another avenue for international engagement. Many waqf properties in India, particularly historical mosques, madrasas, and Sufi shrines, have significant cultural and architectural value. By collaborating with international tourism organizations and heritage conservation bodies, Indian waqf institutions could promote these sites on the global stage, fostering cultural exchange and generating revenue for waqf development.

In the field of academic research, there is ample scope for Indian waqf institutions to collaborate with international universities and research centers. Joint research projects could focus on comparative studies of waqf systems, historical analysis of waqf development, and innovative approaches to waqf revitalization. Such collaborations would not only enhance the global understanding of waqf but also contribute to the development of evidence-based policies and practices.

Lastly, the ongoing reforms in Indian waqf legislation, including the proposed amendments to the Waqf Act, present opportunities for international engagement in the legal and regulatory aspects of waqf management. As India refines its waqf governance framework, there is potential for collaborative efforts with other countries to develop model waqf laws and regulatory standards that could be adapted to different legal and cultural contexts.

In conclusion, the global contributions of Indian waqf institutions are significant and multifaceted. From their historical legacy and vast scale to their ongoing efforts in modernization and reform, Indian waqfs have played a crucial role in shaping the global discourse on Islamic endowments. As they continue to evolve and adapt to changing socio-economic realities, Indian waqf institutions are well-positioned to expand their international engagement and make even greater contributions to the global Islamic economy and social development landscape.

The recognition of Indian waqf institutions on the international stage, their collaborations with global Islamic organizations, and their impact on the Islamic world collectively underscore the importance of Indian waqfs in the global context. Looking ahead, the numerous opportunities for future international engagement promise to further enhance the role of Indian waqf institutions in addressing global challenges and promoting sustainable development through Islamic philanthropic principles.

As the world increasingly recognizes the potential of waqf as a tool for social and economic empowerment, the experiences and innovations of Indian waqf institutions will undoubtedly continue to inform and inspire waqf development efforts around the globe. By leveraging their rich heritage, vast resources, and ongoing reform initiatives, Indian waqfs are poised to make lasting contributions to the global Islamic economy and the broader field of social finance in the years to come.

## References:


1. Abdullah, M. (2020). Islamic endowment (Waqf) in India: Towards poverty reduction of Muslims in the country. Journal of Research in Emerging Markets, 2(2). https://doi.org/10.30585/jrems.v2i2.482

2. Hasnain, S. S. (2017). All you need to know about Waqf and its history in India. OpIndia. https://www.opindia.com/2024/08/all-you-need-to-know-about-waqf-and-its-history-in-india/

3. Husin, A. (2018). Comparative Analysis of Waqf Institutions Governance in India and Singapore. el Barka: Journal of Islamic Economics and Business, 6(2), 257-282.

4. Ihsan, H., & Ayedh, A. (2015). A Comparative Study of Waqf Institutions Governance in India and Malaysia. Intellectual Discourse, Special Issue, 1232-1265.

5. Khan, F. R. (2014). Waqf: An Islamic Instrument of Poverty Alleviation–Bangladesh Perspective. Thoughts on Economics, 23(4), 47-74.

6. Listiana, L. (2020). The Potential Development of Waqf in India Post-COVID-19: A SWOT-TOWS Analysis. International Journal of Islamic Economics and Finance, 3(2), 199-220.

7. Mannan, M. A. (1988). The Economics of Poverty in Islam with Special Reference to Muslim Countries. In M. Iqbal (Ed.), Distributive Justice and Need Fulfillment in an Islamic Economy (pp. 305-335). International Institute of

Islamic Economics.

8.     Owais, M., & Manaf, Z. I. A. (2023). Comparative Analysis of Waqf Institutions Governance in India and Singapore. el Barka: Journal of Islamic Economics and Business, 6(2), 257-282.

9.     Press Information Bureau. (2023). Explainer on Waqf Amendment Bill 2024. Government of India. https://pib.gov.in/PressNoteDetails.aspx?NoteId=152139&ModuleId=3

10.    The Economic Times. (2024). Waqf Act: 'Waqt' for Waqf to change? How the battlelines are drawn. https://economictimes.indiatimes.com/news/india/waqf-act-waqt-for-waqf-to-change-how-the-battlelines-are-drawn/articleshow/112371898.cms

## Chapter 29: Future of Waqf in India

The institution of Waqf in India stands at a critical juncture, poised for significant transformation as it grapples with longstanding challenges and embraces new opportunities for growth and reform. This chapter explores the future landscape of Waqf in India, examining the emerging challenges in Waqf management, identifying opportunities for growth and reform, envisioning a sustainable Waqf system, and outlining a modern framework for Waqf governance.

**Emerging Challenges in Waqf Management:** The management of Waqf properties in India faces several pressing challenges that need to be addressed to ensure the institution's effectiveness and relevance in the 21st century.

**Lack of Transparency and Accountability**

One of the most significant challenges plaguing Waqf management in India is the pervasive lack of transparency and accountability. This issue has allowed for the perpetuation of inefficiencies and corruption within the system (Chishty, 2024). The misuse of Waqf properties by mutawallis (custodians) and the inefficiencies that have prevented Waqf boards from maximizing the value of these assets have been widely acknowledged within the Muslim community.

**Inefficient Property Management**

The inefficient management of Waqf properties has resulted in a significant underutilization of these valuable assets. The Sachar Committee observed that if Waqf properties are put to efficient and marketable use, they could generate a minimum revenue of 10%, amounting to approximately Rs. 12,000 crores per annum. This highlights the vast untapped potential of Waqf properties and the urgent need for improved management practices.

**Legal and Administrative Hurdles**

The current legal framework governing Waqf in India has been criticized for granting arbitrary powers to Waqf Boards, leading to extensive land disputes. For instance, the Tamil Nadu Waqf Board's claim over the entire Thiruchendurai village, which is predominantly Hindu, in September 2022 exemplifies the potential for misuse of these powers. Such incidents underscore the need for a more balanced and transparent legal framework.

## Lack of Modernization

Many Waqf institutions in India continue to operate using outdated management practices and technologies. This lack of modernization hampers their ability to effectively manage properties, maintain accurate records, and adapt to changing socio-economic conditions.

## Encroachment and Property Disputes

Encroachment on Waqf properties and prolonged legal disputes have resulted in the loss of valuable assets. The absence of comprehensive surveys and proper documentation has exacerbated this issue, making it difficult to protect and reclaim Waqf properties.

**Opportunities for Growth and Reform:** Despite the challenges, there are numerous opportunities for growth and reform within the Waqf system in India.

**Legislative Reforms:** The Waqf (Amendment) Bill, 2024, presents a significant opportunity for reform. The bill introduces key changes aimed at increasing transparency and government oversight in Waqf property management. These amendments include:

1. Mandatory verification of all Waqf property claims, involving district magistrates in the oversight process.

2. Registration of Waqf properties with the District Collector's Office, ensuring independent evaluation.

3. Empowering the Central government to order audits of Waqf properties, conducted by auditors appointed by the Comptroller and Auditor-General of India.

4. Ensuring women's representation on the Central Waqf Council and state boards, promoting inclusivity in decision-making.

These legislative changes aim to address the concerns over arbitrary powers and misuse of Waqf properties, potentially leading to a more transparent and accountable system.

## Technological Integration

The integration of modern technology in Waqf management offers immense potential for improvement. Implementing digital record-keeping systems, Geographic Information System (GIS) mapping of Waqf properties, and online platforms for property management and financial transactions can significantly enhance efficiency and transparency.

## Public-Private Partnerships

Exploring public-private partnerships for the development and management of Waqf properties can unlock their economic potential. Such collaborations can bring in expertise, capital, and modern management practices while ensuring the properties' original purpose is maintained.

## Capacity Building and Professional Management

Investing in capacity building programs for Waqf board members, mutawallis, and other stakeholders can enhance their skills in property management, financial planning, and legal compliance. Professionalizing Waqf management by hiring experts in real estate, finance, and law can lead to more efficient and effective administration of Waqf assets.

## Community Engagement and Awareness

Increasing community awareness about the importance of Waqf and its potential for socio-economic development can foster greater participation and support. Engaging the Muslim community in the decision-making process and encouraging their involvement in Waqf development projects can lead to more inclusive and sustainable growth.

 **Vision for a Sustainable Waqf System:** A sustainable Waqf system in India should aim to balance the preservation of religious and cultural heritage with the need for economic viability and social impact. The vision for the future of Waqf in India encompasses several key elements:

## Economic Empowerment

Waqf properties should be leveraged as engines of economic growth for the Muslim community. By developing Waqf assets into productive ventures such as educational institutions, healthcare facilities, and commercial spaces, the system can generate sustainable income streams that can be reinvested in community development initiatives.

## Social Impact

The future Waqf system should prioritize projects that address pressing social issues within the Muslim community, such as education, healthcare, and poverty alleviation. By aligning Waqf initiatives with broader development goals, the institution can play a crucial role in uplifting marginalized sections of society.

## Environmental Sustainability

Incorporating principles of environmental sustainability in the development and management of Waqf properties can ensure their long-term viability. This could include adopting green building practices, investing in renewable energy projects, and promoting sustainable land use.

## Interfaith Harmony

While primarily serving the Muslim community, the Waqf system should also promote interfaith harmony and social cohesion. Developing inclusive spaces and initiatives that benefit the broader society can help foster a sense of unity and mutual respect among different communities.

## Preservation of Cultural Heritage

The future Waqf system should strike a balance between development and the preservation of cultural and historical heritage. Many Waqf properties hold significant cultural value, and their conservation should be an integral part of any development strategy.

## Building a Modern Framework for Waqf Governance

To realize the vision of a sustainable Waqf system, it is crucial to establish a modern framework for Waqf governance. This framework should address the current challenges while incorporating best practices from both Islamic traditions and contemporary management principles.

**Transparent and Accountable Management**: The cornerstone of a modern Waqf governance framework should be transparency and accountability. This can be achieved through:

1. Regular audits and public disclosure of financial statements.

2. Implementation of digital platforms for property management and financial transactions.

3. Establishment of clear performance metrics for Waqf boards and individual properties.

4. Creation of independent oversight committees to monitor Waqf management.

**Professionalization of Waqf Administration**: Professionalizing Waqf administration is crucial for improving efficiency and effectiveness. This can be accomplished by:

1. Hiring qualified professionals with expertise in property management, finance, and law.

2. Implementing performance-based evaluation systems for Waqf administrators.

3. Providing ongoing training and development programs for Waqf board members and staff.

4. Establishing partnerships with academic institutions for research and capacity building in Waqf management.

**Legal and Regulatory Reforms:** To address the current legal challenges and create a more conducive environment for Waqf development, the following reforms should be considered:

1. Streamlining the process for resolving property disputes related to Waqf.

2. Clarifying the roles and responsibilities of various stakeholders in Waqf management.

3. Developing clear guidelines for the development and utilization of Waqf properties.

4. Harmonizing Waqf laws with other relevant legislation to avoid conflicts and ambiguities.

**Innovative Financing Mechanisms:** Exploring innovative financing mechanisms can help unlock the potential of Waqf properties. Some possibilities include:

1. Developing Waqf-based financial instruments, such as Sukuk (Islamic bonds), to raise capital for property development.

2. Establishing Waqf investment funds to pool resources and diversify investments.

3. Exploring crowdfunding platforms to engage the community in Waqf development projects.

4. Implementing revenue-sharing models with private

developers for commercial Waqf properties.

**Community Participation and Representation:** Ensuring meaningful community participation and representation in Waqf governance is essential for its long-term success. This can be achieved through:

1. Establishing community advisory boards for Waqf institutions.

2. Implementing transparent processes for appointing Waqf board members.

3. Conducting regular stakeholder consultations on major Waqf development projects.

4. Encouraging volunteerism and community involvement in Waqf management and development initiatives.

**Technology Integration:** Leveraging technology can significantly enhance the efficiency and transparency of Waqf management. Key areas for technology integration include:

1. Implementing blockchain technology for secure and transparent record-keeping of Waqf properties.

2. Developing mobile applications for easy access to Waqf-related information and services.

3. Utilizing artificial intelligence and data analytics for better decision-making in property management.

4. Creating online platforms for community engagement and crowdsourcing of ideas for Waqf development.

**Collaboration and Knowledge Sharing:** Fostering collaboration and knowledge sharing among Waqf institutions can lead to the adoption of best practices and innovative solutions. This can be facilitated through:

1. Establishing a national Waqf knowledge center to conduct

research and disseminate best practices.

2. Organizing regular conferences and workshops for Waqf administrators and stakeholders.

3. Developing partnerships with international Waqf institutions for knowledge exchange.

4. Creating online forums and communities of practice for Waqf professionals.

In conclusion, the future of Waqf in India holds immense potential for transforming the socio-economic landscape of the Muslim community and contributing to the broader development goals of the nation. By addressing the emerging challenges, seizing opportunities for growth and reform, and implementing a modern governance framework, the Waqf system can evolve into a powerful instrument for sustainable development and social empowerment.

The journey towards realizing this vision will require concerted efforts from various stakeholders, including government bodies, religious leaders, community organizations, and the Muslim community at large. It will also necessitate a delicate balance between preserving the religious and cultural essence of Waqf while adapting to the changing needs of society.

As India moves forward in its development trajectory, a revitalized and well-governed Waqf system can play a crucial role in fostering inclusive growth, promoting interfaith harmony, and contributing to the nation's progress. By embracing transparency, accountability, and innovation, the Waqf institution can not only fulfill its traditional religious and charitable objectives but also emerge as a model for sustainable community development in the 21st century.

**References:**

1.	Chishty, H. S. S. (2024). Reforming Waqf: A Call

for Transparent and Accountable Management for the Welfare of the Muslim Community. Financial Express.

2.    Central Waqf Council. (n.d.). Introduction. Retrieved from https://centralwaqfcouncil.gov.in/content/introduction

3.    Economic Times. (2024). Waqf Act Amendments: Tighter control, more women and non-Muslims members - Five key changes to Waqf law. Retrieved from https://economictimes.indiatimes.com/news/india/waqf-act-amendments-tighter-control-more-women-and-non-muslims-members-five-key-changes-to-waqf-law/articleshow/112373521.cms

4.    Press Information Bureau. (2023). Explainer on Waqf Amendment Bill 2024. Retrieved from https://pib.gov.in/PressNoteDetails.aspx?NoteId=152139&ModuleId=3

5.    The India Forum. (2024). Wakf Reforms, or a Bid to Control Waqf Properties? Retrieved from https://www.theindiaforum.in/law/wakf-reforms-or-bid-control-waqf-properties

# Chapter 30: Conclusion and Recommendations

The institution of waqf has played a significant role in Islamic societies for centuries, serving as a mechanism for charitable endowments and social welfare. However, the management and administration of waqf properties have faced numerous challenges in recent times, necessitating a comprehensive review and reform of the existing legal and administrative frameworks.

One of the key findings is the evolution of waqf legislation in India. The Waqf Act of 1995 marked a significant milestone in the governance of waqf properties, consolidating and amending previous legislation. This Act established a more structured approach to waqf administration, including the formation of Central and State Waqf Boards, and the appointment of Chief Executive Officers for more efficient management.

Despite these legislative efforts, several issues persist in the administration of waqf properties. These include:

1. Mismanagement and corruption: There have been instances of misuse of power by Mutawallis (trustees) and inadequate maintenance of property accounts.

2. Encroachment and property disputes: The lack of effective coordination with local revenue authorities has led to challenges in removing encroachments and resolving property disputes.

3. Inefficient utilization: Many waqf properties generate negligible income, indicating a failure to leverage these assets for community benefit.

4. Legal complexities: The principle of "once a waqf, always a waqf" has led to various disputes and claims, some of which have been deemed perplexing by courts.

5. Lack of diversity in waqf boards: Limited representation of women and non-Muslims in waqf boards has been identified as a concern.

Another significant finding is the distinction between public welfare waqf and family waqf (waqf-alal-aulad). While both are considered charitable under Islamic law, family waqfs have faced challenges in recent times, often being treated as non-charitable institutions under the influence of English law[5].

**Policy Recommendations for Better Waqf Administration:** Based on the identified challenges and evolving needs, the following policy recommendations are proposed for improving waqf administration:

## 1. Enhanced Transparency and Accountability:

- Implement mandatory audits of waqf properties, conducted by auditors appointed by the Comptroller and Auditor-General of India.
- Develop a comprehensive digital database of waqf properties to ensure transparency and ease of management.

## 2. Diversification of Waqf Boards:

- Ensure women's representation on the Central Waqf Council and state boards to promote inclusivity in decision-making.
- Consider including non-Muslim technical experts in waqf management to bring diverse perspectives and expertise.

## 3. Streamlined Property Verification:

- Introduce mandatory verification for all waqf property claims, involving district magistrates in the oversight process.

- Establish clear guidelines for determining the waqf status of properties, addressing the challenges posed by the "once a waqf, always a waqf" principle.

## 4. Legal Reforms:

- Review and potentially amend the non-applicability of the Limitation Act to waqf property claims, which currently allows Waqf Boards to file suits for reclaiming properties without time restrictions.
- Consider establishing an appellate mechanism for Waqf Tribunal decisions to ensure judicial oversight.

## 5. Capacity Building:

- Provide comprehensive training programs for waqf officials, including Mutawallis, on best practices in property management and legal compliance.
- Develop educational initiatives to raise awareness about waqf among the Muslim community and the general public.

## 6. Economic Utilization:

- Encourage innovative approaches to utilize waqf properties for generating sustainable income, such as leasing for commercial purposes while maintaining the charitable intent.
- Explore public-private partnerships for developing and managing waqf properties.

## 7. Dispute Resolution:

- Strengthen the Waqf Tribunals by providing them with adequate resources and trained personnel.
- Establish alternative dispute resolution mechanisms, such as mediation, to resolve waqf-related conflicts efficiently.

**8. Inter-agency Coordination:** Foster better coordination between Waqf Boards, revenue authorities, and local governments to address issues of encroachment and property registration.

**9. Preservation of Historical Waqf Properties:** Develop specific guidelines and allocate resources for the preservation and restoration of historically significant waqf properties.

**10. Regular Review and Reform:** Establish a mechanism for periodic review of waqf laws and administration to ensure they remain relevant and effective in changing socio-economic contexts.

**The Role of Community in Protecting Waqf**

The protection and proper management of waqf properties is not solely the responsibility of government bodies and Waqf Boards. The Muslim community, and indeed the broader society, have a crucial role to play in safeguarding these valuable assets. The following strategies can enhance community involvement in waqf protection:

1. Awareness and Education:

Community leaders, religious scholars, and educational institutions should work together to raise awareness about the significance of waqf properties. This includes educating people about the religious, social, and economic importance of waqf, as well as the legal frameworks governing them. Public lectures, seminars, and educational materials can be used to disseminate this information widely.

2. Community Vigilance:

Local communities can form vigilance committees to monitor waqf properties in their areas. These committees can act as watchdogs, reporting any encroachments, misuse, or neglect of waqf properties to the relevant authorities. This grassroots-level monitoring can significantly complement the efforts of official bodies.

3. Volunteerism and Maintenance:

Community members can contribute their time and skills to maintain and improve waqf properties. This could include organizing clean-up drives, assisting in minor repairs, or providing professional services (such as legal or architectural advice) pro bono. Such involvement not only helps in maintaining the properties but also fosters a sense of ownership and responsibility within the community.

4. Documentation and Record-Keeping:

Community members, particularly those with relevant expertise, can assist in documenting and digitizing records related to waqf properties. This can include historical documents, property details, and usage records. Accurate and accessible documentation is crucial for protecting waqf properties from potential disputes or encroachments.

5. Advocacy and Legal Support:

Community organizations and individuals can advocate for better waqf management at various levels of government. This can include lobbying for favorable policies, raising issues of mismanagement or encroachment with relevant authorities, and providing legal support in cases involving waqf properties.

6. Fundraising and Financial Support:

While waqf properties are meant to be self-sustaining, many face financial challenges. Community members can organize fundraising campaigns to support the maintenance and development of waqf properties, especially those that provide essential services like mosques, schools, or hospitals.

7. Collaboration with Waqf Boards:

Establishing strong connections between community members and state Waqf boards is essential for effective waqf management. Community leaders should actively engage with Waqf boards, providing input on local needs and challenges, and participating in decision-making processes where possible.

## 8. Interfaith Dialogue:

Engaging in interfaith dialogue can help build understanding and support for waqf properties among non-Muslim communities. This can be particularly important in areas where waqf properties are located in mixed communities or face challenges due to lack of awareness.

## 9. Use of Technology:

Tech-savvy community members can contribute by developing digital platforms or applications that help in mapping, monitoring, and managing waqf properties. This can include creating databases, reporting systems, or even blockchain-based solutions for transparent management.

## 10. Succession Planning:

Community leaders should encourage and assist in proper succession planning for family waqfs (waqf-alal-aulad). This can help prevent disputes and ensure the continued charitable use of these properties as intended by the original donors.

By actively engaging in these areas, the community can play a vital role in protecting and enhancing the value of waqf properties, ensuring they continue to serve their intended charitable purposes for generations to come.

## Final Thoughts on the Social and Legal Dimensions of Waqf

The institution of waqf represents a unique intersection of religious, social, and legal dimensions in Islamic societies. Its evolution and current challenges reflect broader societal changes and the complexities of managing religious endowments in modern, secular states.

From a social perspective, waqf has historically played a crucial role in providing public goods and services, from educational institutions to healthcare facilities. This social function remains relevant today, particularly in addressing gaps in public welfare systems. However, the full potential of waqf as a tool for social development is often unrealized due to management inefficiencies and legal constraints.

Legally, the management of waqf presents unique challenges. The principle of perpetuity in waqf, while ensuring long-term charitable impact, can sometimes conflict with modern property laws and economic efficiency considerations. The tension between religious law (Sharia) and secular state laws in managing waqf properties is an ongoing issue in many countries, including India.

The recent amendments and proposed changes to waqf laws in India reflect an attempt to balance traditional principles with modern administrative needs. The emphasis on transparency, accountability, and efficient management is a step in the right direction. However, care must be taken to ensure that these reforms do not dilute the fundamental charitable intent of waqf or alienate the Muslim community from their religious endowments.

The role of the state in waqf administration is another critical aspect. While state oversight is necessary to prevent mismanagement and ensure compliance with broader legal frameworks, excessive government control can be perceived as interference in religious affairs. Striking the right balance requires careful consideration and ongoing dialogue between the state, religious authorities, and the community.

The concept of family waqf (waqf-alal-aulad) presents its own set of challenges. While it serves important social functions within Muslim families, its treatment under modern legal systems has often been problematic. Recognizing the charitable nature of family waqfs, as intended in Islamic law, while preventing misuse for tax evasion or circumvention of inheritance laws, remains a complex issue.

Looking forward, the revitalization of waqf as an institution requires a multi-faceted approach. This includes legal reforms, improved management practices, community engagement, and innovative financial models. The use of modern financial instruments, such as waqf-based sukuk (Islamic bonds), and the application of professional asset management techniques to waqf properties, could significantly enhance their economic impact.

Education and awareness about waqf, both within the Muslim community and in broader society, are crucial. Understanding the historical significance and contemporary relevance of waqf can foster greater support for its protection and development.

In conclusion, waqf remains a vital institution with significant potential for social good. However, realizing this potential in the 21st century requires a delicate balancing act between preserving its religious and charitable essence and adapting to modern legal, economic, and social realities. The ongoing efforts to reform and revitalize waqf administration in India and other countries offer valuable lessons and opportunities for harnessing this ancient institution for contemporary social benefit.

The future of waqf lies in embracing transparency, efficiency, and community involvement while staying true to its core principles of perpetual charity and social welfare. As societies continue to grapple with issues of inequality and social development, the waqf system, properly managed and utilized, can serve as a powerful tool for community empowerment and sustainable development.

## References

1. ABVP. (2024, October 1). Waqf – History and Evolution. https://www.abvp.org/article/waqf-history-and-evolution

2. Economic Times. (2024, August 8). Waqf Act Amendments: Tighter control, more women and non-Muslims members - five key changes to Waqf law. https://economictimes.indiatimes.com/news/india/waqf-act-amendments-tighter-control-more-women-and-non-muslims-members-five-key-changes-to-waqf-law/articleshow/112373521.cms

3. Press Information Bureau. (2023, July 24). Explainer on Waqf Amendment Bill 2024. https://pib.gov.in/PressNoteDetails.aspx?NoteId=152139&ModuleId=3

4. India Tomorrow. (2024, February 22). Community vigilance, awareness key to protect Waqf assets: Call from Bangalore workshop. https://indiatomorrow.net/2024/02/22/community-vigilance-awareness-key-to-protect-waqf-assets-call-from-bangalore-workshop/

5. Sadique, M. A., Ansari, A. H., Hingun, M., & Hasan, A. (n.d.). Socio-Legal Significance of Family Waqf in Islamic Law: Its Degeneration and Revival. IIUM Law Journal. https://journals.iium.edu.my/iiumlj/index.php/iiumlj/article/download/275/198/978

6. Wikipedia. (2024, November 5). Waqf. https://en.wikipedia.org/wiki/Waqf

7. Ansari, R. A. (n.d.). Citizens' Participation in Protecting Waqf Properties. Radiance Weekly. https://radianceweekly.net/citizens-participation-in-protecting-waqf-properties/

8. Business Standard. (2024, August 5). Decoded: How is a Waqf created, and what are the powers of Waqf Board? https://www.business-standard.com/india-news/decoded-how-is-a-waqf-created-and-what-are-the-powers-of-waqf-board-124080500469_1.html

9. Jamaat-e-Islami Hind. (n.d.). Muslim community must

unite to safeguard Waqf properties: Syed Sadatullah Hussaini. https://jamaateislamihind.org/eng/muslim-community-must-unite-to-safeguard-waqf-properties-syed-sadatullah-hussaini/

## THE END

www.ingramcontent.com/pod-product-compliance
Lightning Source LLC
Chambersburg PA
CBHW061033250726
48653CB00001B/72